The Music of
The Incredible
String Band

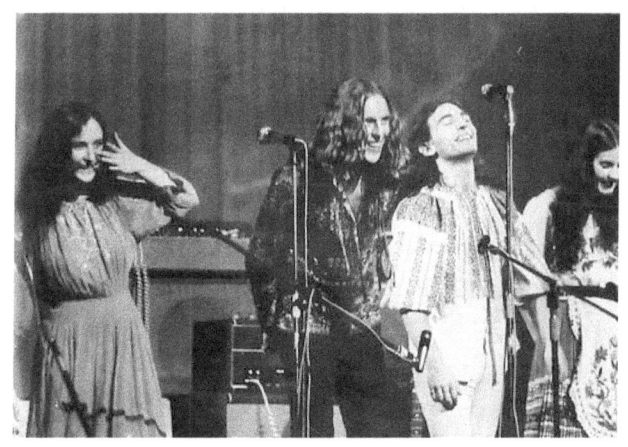

By Chris Wade

The Music of The Incredible String Band by Chris Wade

PUBLISHED BY WISDOM TWINS BOOKS
wisdomtwinsbooks.weebly.com

This edition released in 2019

CONTENTS

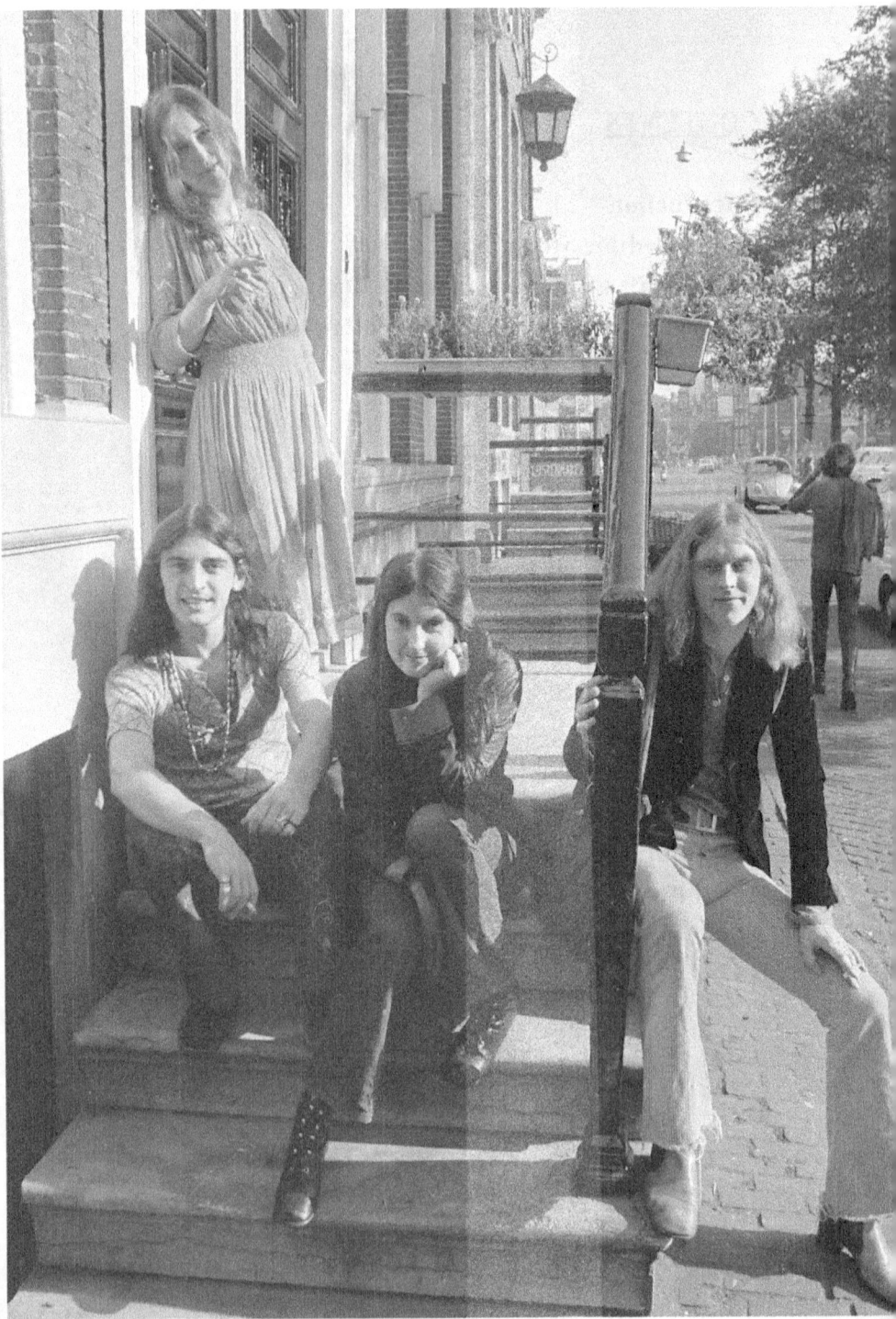

Introduction

The Incredible String Band. Those four words to some will mean very little, but to many, and to be perfectly honest a growing number of newer generations, the band are one of the most sublime, original and innovative outfits ever to have emerged on to the music scene. Their unique brand of often avant-garde music which transcended genres and crossed previously forbidden borders somehow made into the mainstream. Influencing everyone from The Beatles to Led Zeppelin, the core iconic members of the ISB, Mike Heron and Robin Williamson, are today elder statesmen of psychedelic folk, gods of what some call acid folk. But of course, like with any great genre innovators, such terms as "acid" and "psychedelic" are likely to be met with indifference. As Heron once noted on a BBC documentary, they were making the music they felt like making, and such tags today must seem, to him at least, rather daft. But then, it's perfectly natural to sum up a sound with a tag, and for a band as often out-there and singular as the ISB, clinging to any genre or sub genre can actually be comforting to those not in the understanding. After all, the world of the Incredible String Band can at first seem to be a strange place. That is of course until you get settled in. And even then it's still strange. They were certainly doing their own thing in a time when most bands were cloning each other in a bid to get a hit single. In fact, almost perversely, some of the biggest bands of the day got more than a hint of inspiration from the ISB, especially if you ask Robin himself. "It went in quite a few directions," he said. "I think one of the directions that you might be interested to look at was, like, the Rolling Stones' Satanic Majesties Request. I would think that that is quite String Band influenced. Also some of the

Beatles' work around about the time of Sgt. Pepper and immediately thereafter has got faint touches and both of them used to come and see us play."

So why then, with such a brilliant and varied discography, where the lads took in every style they could, played every instrument that came their way and wrote about almost every subject possible, has their work been side lined almost, now little more than a note in the history of pop and the landscape of 1960s music? Sure they have their admirers, and as I said it seems to be growing among young people, but I don't feel they have been properly recognised, especially by the mainstream media, as the true innovative force they were, like their contemporaries Nick Drake or Fairport Convention. There would be no psychedelic folk if not for the ISB, no acid folk, no fusion folk, none of the countless modern imitators turning up on indi-labels these days. We have a lot to thank the ISB for. Even Stairway to Heaven was a direct nod to them!

So, is this book going to magically put them forward as one of the 1960s' stand out artists? In short, no, but then they already are to some people. But this book may point people in the right direction, shed light on the colourful sounds they made and highlight the influence they have had down the decades. They have brought many people a lot of joy, me being one of them. I hope this little book brings some joy to others too.

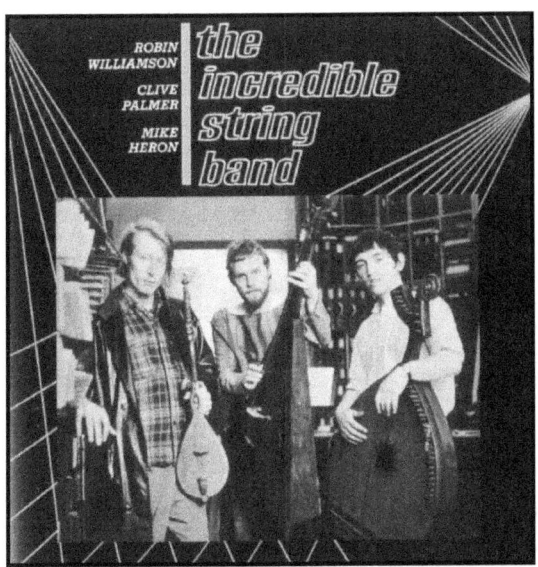

The Incredible String Band (1966)

The Scottish folk scene in the mid sixties was seeing a similar sort of boom as it was in England, especially in London and all over the UK for that matter. In New York it was the same, the cafes and bars of Greenwich Village were full of emerging young talent like Bob Dylan, who, armed only with a voice and an acoustic guitar, were bringing much deeper content to the art of the song. Taking in traditional folk tools and bringing them up to date, folk fusion and eventually folk rock were slowly being invented. Amidst the resurgence, Edinburgh based songwriter Archie Fisher ran a weekly folk club at the Crown bar, and here many of the top folk players of the day regularly entertained the gathered punters. You would often catch Bert Jansch playing and on some nights, a rather interesting duo consisting of Clive Palmer and Robin Williamson.

"In 1963 I went up to Edinburgh, where I started going to a bar with a folk club in it called the Crown," Palmer recalled to Mojo magazine. "One night I saw this young, red-faced local with a big sweater on playing beautiful, very simple Scottish songs on guitar. It was Robin Williamson.'

Robin had previously been playing solo gigs on guitar when he met Clive, a particularly strong banjo player and the two fused together their ideas. Although a traditionalist at heart, Robin knew he could introduce his own ideas while still retaining an "old folk" sensibility.

"It (Scotland) had an interesting scene," Williamson said. "Because it had an existing tradition going on that was neglected enough for it to be quite wild.... The tradition hadn't been tempered with at all in Scotland. So it wasn't a revival, exactly, it was still all there. As it was in Ireland. It had never gone away. So when we came in with a new take on it, we were taking it right from the source, rather than from the revival."

In 1965, a young man by the name of Joe Boyd walked in and caught the boys in action. He was working as a talent scout for Elektra Records at the time and took a mental note that these were an act to look out for. "Scotland and Edinburgh in general were epicentres of a kind of drug culture in the 1960s," Boyd recalled. "In which a lot of people took acid, a lot of people smoked dope in way that didn't exist in England in the folk scene. People smoked dope maybe but there weren't too many mind blown folk singers." He clearly saw the advancements culturally and musically already apparent in the Edinburgh folk scene. "Robin and Clive were distorting Scottish music," Boyd added. "Completely unlike anything I'd ever heard before. It had this real freshness, genuinely human

British and echoes of Scottish traditional music, and echoes of Eastern music and echoes of William Blake and god knows what in this thing."

Boyd saw them at point blank range, playing in a pub to a crowd of 30. Clive had a limp Boyd remembered and appeared older than his years, while Williamson was "graceful and relaxed." Meeting Robin after the show, he was convinced he had found the star he was looking for.

Although going down well in the clubs, the duo felt the need to expand their sound and placed an advert looking for a rhythm guitarist. Mike Heron, a young musician from close by, stepped forward to audition and won them over. He had previously been working at a law firm when he chanced upon the two ragamuffins.

"I was very kind of straight and living with my parents," Heron recalled on the BBC. "And Robin was a fully fledged beatnik at the time. He introduced me to the world of white washed rooms and books of Jack Kerouac on the table. And so he kind of interested me... all that artistic stuff that hadn't touched me in the rock scene... or in the accountant's office." Heron later recalled he couldn't think of anything else to do and joked that his level of commitment on becoming an accountant was "pathetic".

"There are some people in this world," he told Beat Instrumental, "who get high making out accounts. It's very weird to dig it but that's the thing that does it for them. I chucked up accounting half to be a musician and half to be a beatnik. Most of the grooviest people around at that time were beatniks."

The son of a teacher, Heron had been in a few bands, such as The Saracens in late 1965 before realising that the rules needed to be changed and the strict conventions of music were becoming rather dull. While Heron had flirted with rock and roll, Williamson had originally wanted to be a writer, modelling his style on Kerouac's. Tied between the free form literary movements of the 50s and the Celtic traditions, Williamson's literary aspirations found a medium in song. Robin loved the ethereal purity of acoustic instruments, "in the days before the synthesizers" as he put it. "I suppose what I was trying to do was open up the whole subject of folk music into a different and wider sphere. Not necessarily a rock sphere, but more of a sort of literary and world music sphere." Heron says they were basically cobbling together a sound they wanted to hear themselves from quite early on, while Williamson clearly wanted to get away from the technique aspect and go back to an almost child like, wide eyed innocent approach towards the instrument in question, like "naïve painting" as he has often described it.

The trio took the confident name The Incredible String Band, performing weekly at Clive Palmer's own Incredible Folk Club in Glasgow. The club itself was housed on the fourth floor of a building in Sauchiehall Street. Basically an illegal drinking establishment, as there was no fire exit to speak of and only an elevator which went straight up to the club, the trio soon became the house band for the venue. "We started at midnight and finished at 7 o'clock in the morning," Williamson recalled.

"All the gangs used to fight amongst themselves," Heron remembered. "While the bouncers carried swords down their trouser legs. We were the resident group and would usually sit there terrified. It wasn't the ideal aesthetic environment for us."

If truth be told, they were actually finding it hard to get booked elsewhere, and London in particular, where the influential folk figure Ewan MacColl wasn't a big fan of what the boys were doing. But having a residency meant regular money coming in, "a do it yourself version of employment" as Robin beautifully put it once. Sparking against Williamson's fascination with tradition, Mike was certainly more rock and pop oriented. With Palmer's "Edwardian banjo" to boot, there is little wonder why a folk purist might feel threatened by such a hybrid of styles.

Now the head of Elektra Records in London, Joe Boyd returned in March of 1966 and signed the band. They had almost taken a deal with Transatlantic, but a better offer from Elektra convinced them to go with Boyd. (It was in fact an extra 50 pounds that convinced them). The actual night he met the new line up was coincidentally the same night the police closed the club down, calling the venue a fire hazard (which it quite clearly was) and the boys invited Boyd to their house to play some more of their songs the next morning. "Kids and dope everywhere," Boyd recalled. "Flowered skirts and blouses, velvet cloaks, silk scarves and muddy shoes, all infused with the scent of patchouli." Boyd was impressed with the new recruit Mike, who was teasing the other two band members, slapping his knee in delight.

They had recently recorded some demos on a cassette and given it to Boyd, who then it took the tape to the label. The stand out track was clearly October Song, which was pretty much the deal breaker for the chaps at Elektra. Sessions were arranged to record a full album, and the full repertoire was laid down in one weekend according to Boyd. All three men gathered round a couple of microphones and cut their live set speedily and the rest is history. The budget was 100 pounds according to Boyd, but that didn't really matter, as the young producer recalled the album being very easy to record, seeing as the band already had their songs well oiled to start with.

"He (Boyd) didn't interfere really," Williamson said of recording with him. "He was more of an enabler than a director. He used to sort of get you in there... just let you get on with it. And I think it's impossible to underestimate the contribution of John Wood, the engineer. He was one of the first guys to have all the modern multi tracking facilities in Britain that I know of. Early on, the first record was all standing around one microphone. So that was a 1950s technique."

Although ISB devotees probably wouldn't instantly recommend the first album as a starting point for a newcomer to the band, it probably is a really good place to begin if you're thinking of delving into the whole catalogue. After all, the records do get a bit more far out by the later period of the 1960s and the instrumentation, writing and arrangements are something one must get used to rather than instantly be thrown into the deep end of.

The debut begins with a lovely Heron number, Maybe Someday, a brilliant lyric over a gorgeous folk melody. Heron longs for his lost girl, and Williamson backs up nicely with his trademark high harmony vocals, contrasting against Mike's warmer classic tones. A chorus this strong is a brilliant place to start and it pulls you straight into the broad palette ahead.

October Song, quite possibly the band's best known cut, is the second track and it's easy to see why this song has become something of a folk classic. Ignoring the fact that it was, of course, a favourite of Dylan's back in the sixties, it's a song that never ages, doesn't date at all and is as sweet now as I am sure it was back in 1966. As the tortured violin of the opening song dies out, Williamson's sublime ballad fades in and instantly enters the heart. Although often unconventional vocal-wise, here his voice is utterly unforgettable and extremely powerful, the poetry within it picturesque and the arrangement floatingly soothing. It's as if, like Robin hints in the lyrics, the song is not his own, but offered to him from somewhere above. You really do get lost amidst it, in a daydreaming place you really don't want to leave. Same goes for Heron's lovely The Tree, a summery, breezy feel-good track and surely one of Mike's finest. The album continues in this way; it's easily approachable yet colourful and full of character, and the slight contrast between Heron and Williamson's styles is, although apparent, actually at its smoothest and most seamless. Sure, when the duo started experimenting with styles more in the latter part of the decade, Heron's songs seemed much more grounded than Robin's. But Heron did once note, perhaps with a hint of humour that he was "just a boring old songwriter." It's clear even here though that he preferred the straight-on approach to song, engaging the listener immediately with a warmth and depth many singer-songwriters would die for. It's also telling to note that Heron has often said this is one of his personal favourite ISB records, and it's easy to see why. It's undiluted and straight from the heart, not distracted or influenced by success, formulas or a public's perception of the band as an entity.

Robin's Dandelion Blues finishes off side one, with fine finger picking and vocals. We hear shades of Woody Guthrie here, and it's fair to say that this era of ISB fits right in with the emerging modern folk style that was flirting with, and in some cases dominating the charts that year; people like Dylan, Al Stewart, Donovan in his denim phase perhaps and even Simon and Garfunkel. This track has the ISB on a fairly commercial and approachable form, but still, its straight forward fashion is no bad thing. Those who only know ISB as mind bending freak out hippies (which I still don't think they are anyway!) should check this out. This could have been recorded last week.

Heron starts the second side brilliantly with an early example of his very original radiant style, How Happy I Am. However, the line "I won't feel sad till the whiskey's gone" indicates that not all is as happy as it seems. But our narrator is not just going to sit and wait for this girl to come back from doing whatever she pleases, he's going to drink while doing so. As with numerous Heron numbers, here the surface exterior is light and jovial, but the under current is perhaps a little more complex. Elsewhere we see pre echoes of classic ISB. In title alone, Smoke Shovelling Song makes you think of Deep South America, but its slightly quirky arrangement hints at 67/68 ISB.

Upon release, the record proved popular, steadily earning them a cult following and among other plaudits, a position in Melody Maker's reader's poll as "Best Folk Album of the Year." The US sleeve (not pictured at the start of this chapter) is in my opinion a better cover than the one us Brits got, but either one summed up the rusty, raw feel of the album perfectly. The whole record makes you want to check your shoes to make sure they're not full of sand.

After the release of the album however, the trio went their separate ways. Palmer left for a hippy trip to India, growing tired of the psychedelic direction the band were starting to head towards in late 66, first hitchhiking to Afghanistan and returning years later in the 1970s, making his mark on the Cornish folk scene.

"Quite honestly, I couldn't stand the music they were writing," recalled Palmer years later, although you should perhaps take these words with a pinch of salt. "Also, I was a beatnik and could never have got into the middle-class hippy thing. I can remember a row before a TV appearance when Robin asked me to get a haircut, and to stop mixing with people who smoked dope. People used to say you could write fantastic music on acid, but it didn't affect me at all. LSD was rubbish."

Robin however, with his girlfriend Christina "Licorice" McKechnie went to Morocco. In fact Robin hadn't planned to even return to

Britain at all, leaving Mike behind, who in turn formed a new group of his own called Rock Bottom and the Deadbeats. The Incredible String Band story looked to be over already.

But Williamson was to return after all. It was all very well planning a trip to Morocco, but he hadn't even thought of realistic accommodation or how he might earn a living. He thought, in his own words, that he might just live under a tree. "That was my plan, sit under a tree somewhere and learn Arabic flute," he said. Nice sounding idea that is.

But running out of funds, he and Licorice returned, albeit armed with a host of exotic and colourful Moroccan instruments they didn't quite understand. Heron, glad to see the return of his comrade, decided the pair of them should become a musical duo. And Joe Boyd, still very impressed with the music, was appointed manager.

Chapter two was about to begin.

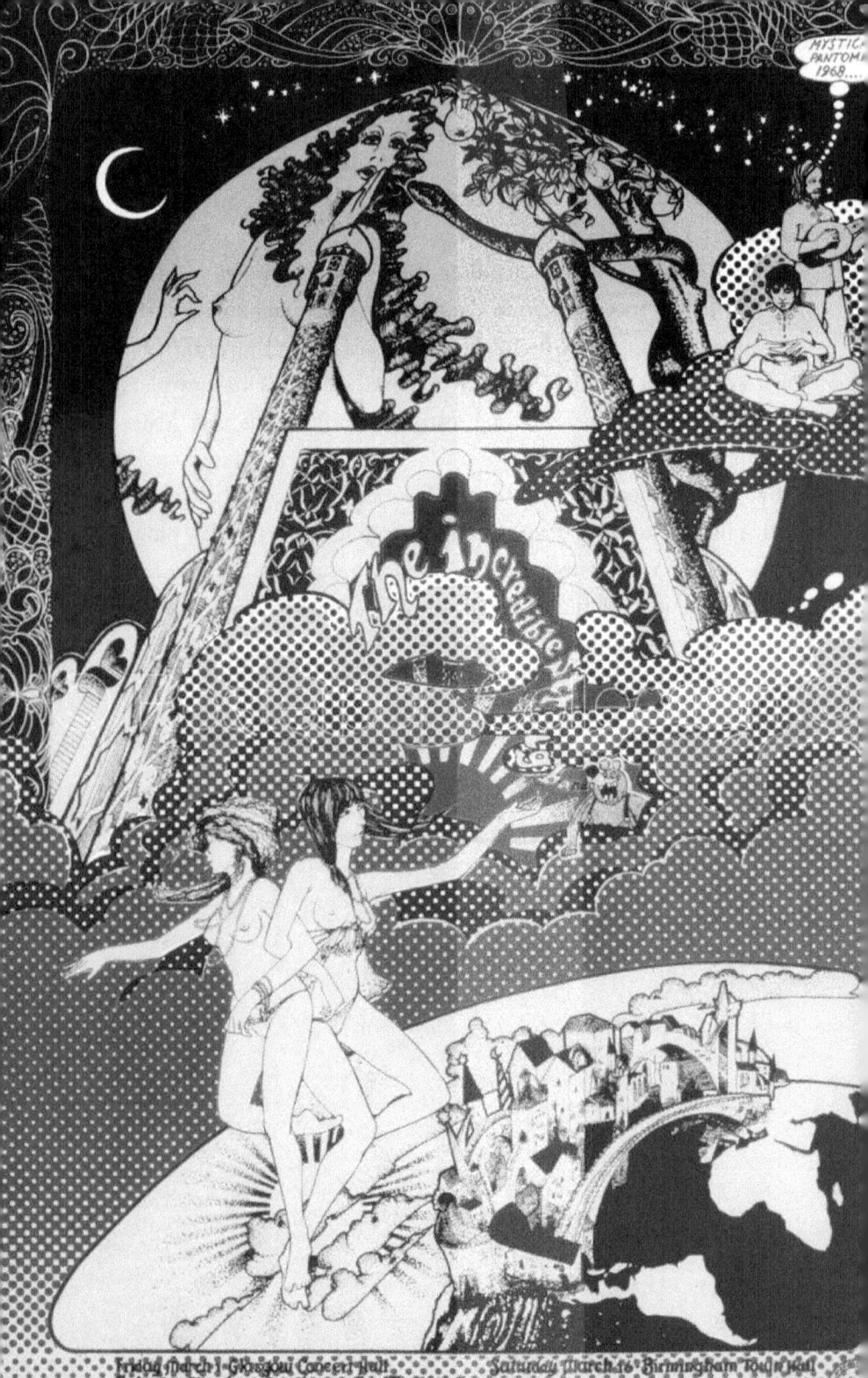

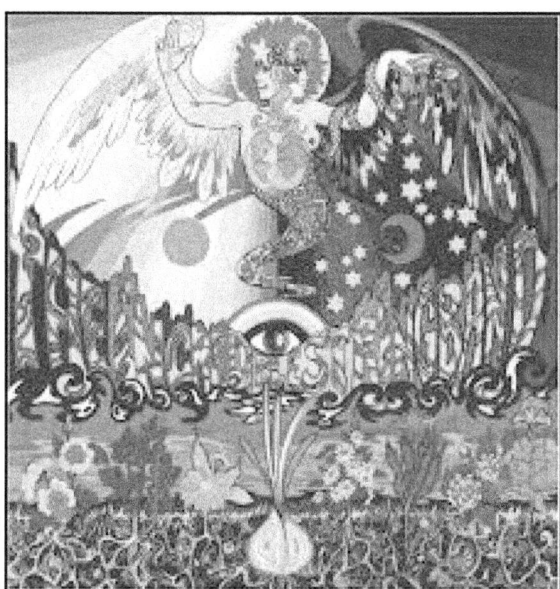

The 5000 Spirits or the Layers of the Onion (1967)

"We'll have a go with this, make a noise on this, clang on this, thump on that, squeak on the other."
– Robin Williamson, Folk Britannia, BBC

It's fair to say there was a dramatic shift in sound when Robin and Mike recorded their second album, The 5000 Spirits or the Layers of the Onion. The new music was much freer, it was wonderfully experimental and definitely representative of the typical sound one might associate with the late 60s drug culture scene. Boyd called them "drug culture pioneers," but how much influence and effect did drugs have on the lads and their new sound, and what does Mike think of the theory that tied together experimental music and experimental drugs?

Mike Heron: "The point to be made is that I don't really think it was the drugs that brought it about, it was just a common factor, people sat around listening to music, it wasn't a pro-drug thing, it just happened that that was the invisible catalyst that stirred it all together. One of the main things too is that pop bands hadn't really quite broken through at that time, it was clubs like UFO and places like that, and more the psychedelic thing, which was a bit after that, that made it possible for rock bands to sing songs that people would listen to. Even the Beatles when they started, it was that kind of music you went to a dance and you either danced to it or you didn't. You didn't sit down on the floor and kind of go "Ah, Crikey ... Great words!" and actually listen to the songs! So what we did was listenable too, the lyrics and the mixture of music and all that kind of stuff, and that was what really attracted us to do it. That's why we came up through folk rather than rock, because I basically came from rock, my roots are rock, but I was playing that kind of music and nobody cared much about the lyrics, and I discovered that if you played folk people actually listened to what you were saying (and Dylan came around about that time too) and your songs could be rated as songs rather than just music you could dance to or not."

A good point to illuminate is the fact that Boyd wanted to take the ISB out of the folk scene, with its strict rules and cultural and sonic limitations, which no doubt changed the perspective on the band's music from the outside at least. As a result, the ISB were embraced and received by the alternative scene, and the album was rated even more highly than the first (and selling 10 times as many copies according to Boyd). But this was not merely due to a cultural shift in the band's audience, it was also musical. This album is rich, totally characteristic of their ability to blend the beauty of Celtic, Indian and traditional folk styles, a combination which effortlessly creates a new genre of its own. World Music perhaps? It resulted in the band becoming key figures in the advancement of popular music and even getting to number 25 on the UK charts, which when considering the type of material on this album, is pretty remarkable. The reviewers were ecstatic to say the least ("Better than The Beatles!" etc.) and the band continued playing clubs and venues to promote the record, including the UFO Club, which Boyd also ran. It was the point where they came into their own, when the ISB sound became a genre of its own.

Recorded in very early 1967 at London's Sound Techniques with Boyd again, the lads were joined by Pentangle's Danny Thompson on double bass and Licorice herself providing vocals and percussion. John "Hoppy" Hopkins, the man who famously co-founded the International Times, and was in fact one of the key figures of the 1960s underground music scene, was rumoured to have played piano on the album.

"Yes it was me," John told me by email. "All 16 bars of it." Demonstrating a strong element of eccentricity to this day, he added "unfortunately I have just broken my leg and will be out of the loop for a while. Sorry to disappoint." Still, it was very much Mike and Robin's own little world and Boyd enjoyed being a part of it, loving the recording process immensely. He was also charmed by the new material, the strange lyrics, rich melodies, and the "off the wall" ideas they kept coming up with.

Chinese White opens the album, a now classic favourite among the fans. A Mike Heron oddity for sure, it shows him at his quirkiest, lyrically and vocally. Robin's screeching violin could have been played by The Velvet Underground's John Cale (who co-incidentally appeared on Mike's first solo album, Smiling Men with Bad Reputations), under laying the lyric but somehow never threatening to take over it. A line like "will your magic Christmas tree be shining all around," could only work in an ISB song for sure, but its charm and innocence only warms the heart. The second number is Robin's wild Americana style slide-fest No Sleep Blues, where a restless Williamson rants in a Dylan-esque manner, rather like one of the beat writers he so idolised in his youth, while Heron puts his unique stamp on the song with some brilliant backing vocals. The sitar, played here by Nazir Jairazbhoy (an instrument later mastered by Heron himself of course) and the flute also dance wildly together to add some nice touches. Clearly, the more conventional blues rhythm is something we may have heard before, but the added flute and sitar lines are what make such a potentially conventional song innovative in its inspired collage of cultural sounds. Then there's the words of course. "The dawn keeps on sneaking up when it thinks I'm not looking" must surely be one of Robin's most tortured and paranoid lines. With lyrics so usually associated with dreams, surreal fables and child like fairytales, it's odd and also refreshing to hear such a twitchy, restless neurotic monologue, a rant you'd normally expect from some speed freak.

As soon as it begins, Painting Box sounds special. Later covered by Julie Felix (who also did a duet of it with the ISB lads on her TV show), the original album version, written and sung by Mike, is an exquisite number, made all the more sweeter in the wake of Williamson's jagged beat poet riffing on the previous track. There is a charm about this type of Heron song, a lovely naivety, and with

Licorice's perfect backing vocals behind Mike's voice, the song enters an almost child-like euphoric area rarely conjured up in music. The play off between the flute and guitar after the chorus takes the song into an even wilder and more wonderful area too, while lyrics like "baby raindrops playing on the window" could have been written by Lewis Carroll or one of the classic children's writers. "Lately when I look into my painting box, I seem to pick the colours of you," hints at the lingering sense of love entering the body, as ones self becomes besotted with the object of affection. It's like the mind giving itself into the heart; sentimental yes, but also perfectly executed. Heron also shines on The Hedgehog Song, another cult favourite which he still plays to this day, while his bright cheeriness clashes brilliantly with Williamson at his most undisciplined on tracks like The Mad Hatter's Song. One Robin stand out is Way Back in the 1960s, where our narrator curiously looks back on that most decadent decade as an older man, lamenting a time when people "made their own entertainment" and even "went to the pictures." Once again, these kind of lyrics can only work in an ISB song, or be written by them for that matter. But the music floats from one style to another, changing speeds, tempos and rhythms as quick as possible, carrying the words along with it. Somehow, even if some of the lyrics are almost too obvious, and the melodies seem too wild, it all works brilliantly. Why can't more bands have such a fearless love for the free form and the experimental, the welding of ideas and styles?

Williamson then lures us into hazy Celtic mystery with the brilliant The Eyes of Fate, and once again it refuses to stick to one melody. But Mad Hatter's Song is quite possibly the album's strongest track, and the interplay between guitar and sitar is once again inspired. While from 1966 onwards The Beatles played with Indian sounds, the

ISB dove right in and mixed it into their own melting pot of magic. Donovan had also done this on his Sunshine Superman album, but although the results were nice on his 1966 classic, they were often not as listenable or inspired as the ISB's take on the idea, nor any where near as imaginative. Simply using the Indian sounds is not always enough, but using them to enhance an already fantastic melody is something else. You would think that the boogie woogie section, which suddenly invades the song at 2 or so minutes into its duration, would jar awkwardly just as you had been getting used to the dreamy "do what you like" melody. But of course it doesn't. With the ISB, you get used to these unconventional shifts in tone and sound, and accept them. In fact, the more imagery and ideas they fit into one song the better. It becomes wildly addictive, discovering a new sea of tones you could swim around in all day.

The haunting My Name is Death is another chilling Williamson ballad, his vocals once again perfect, his strums deep and full, lyrics that conjure images of a stark, dark, Dystopian valley, as the cold reaper himself comes to collect the dead. But there are still very conventional moments on this album, most notably on First Girl I Loved, a very touching ballad where Robin wonders what happened to the girl he adored as a child and suggests with sadness that she has become little more than "a grown up female stranger." There was no sex with this fair maiden, but they "must have made love a thousand times". Has young innocent love ever been put sweeter than that?

With moments like this, swimming deeply in idyllic British poetry, why is it that the band are remembered, and cemented in fact, as just a typical product of the drug culture? Sure, they get far out from time to time, but tying all these various ideas together was a grounded sense of human understanding, a sensibility of love and a purity rarely seen in popular music. It's positive, never dark, not drugged out and scary, nor frightened and edgy. The ISB's world is full of colour and sunshine.

So what of the cosmic album title?

"I thought up most of the String Band titles," Robin later told Swing Time Magazine. "... and they were just things that seemed like good little phrases. It was about as much as that. If you want to get really deep about it, it seemed to be a symbol of consciousness. You know, you either think of it of layers and layers and layers of onion or thousands of voices. So it seemed like a good title at the time. A lot of the String Band lyrics at that time were almost deliberately ambiguous; they were not intended to be direct communications particularly. They were things that you could get your own interpretations out of and that was something that we felt very strongly about. It was almost like word-jazz. It was more like things you could get ideas from, get your own images. One of the things that I felt perhaps I contributed at that time was the idea of using a variety of different kinds of instruments to colour the sound, because at that time there were just the two of us in the band and I had acquired a number of exotic instruments and Mike was getting into sitar and so forth. We were just using a whole lot of instruments and I began writing songs that would allow a variety of changes within one song. See, it would start in one kind of style and use the appropriate musical style for this piece of the song, then it might require some other kind of piece, you know. So, it was, like, things that were strung together with different moods and different flavours thrown in there and I think in a way this was the first sort of attempts at what might be now called 'fusion music'. I think we were the only band who was doing anything like that."

Having the freedom to interpret songs how you choose to is a most refreshing thing when dealing with a songwriter. So many modern songs are too clearly defined, it's either a love song, a song of lost love, or a song that's only message is that dancing is an enjoyable activity. Lyrics are too obvious, too clear, so much so in fact that they tend to become clichéd parodies of themselves. You've heard them a thousand times it seems. But with free form "jazz poetry", the listener is freed of any pre-conceived concepts. Listen to the words, divulge in them, delight in them, and enjoy them. We are given language as a gift and yet we don't use it as we should. It seems hat the ISB, and Robin in particular here, is asking us to appreciate the words we have been given, enjoy the sound of them and the way they can delicately roll off the tongue.

The striking psychedelic cover art also deserves more than a passing mention. Boyd wanted a strong cover to attract attention, and perhaps to appeal to the alternative music fans, so he hired the artistic team "The Fool" consisting of Maijke and Simon Posthuma (the team had also painted the side wall on The Beatles' famous Apple boutique). Now it's almost the clichéd epitome of psychedelic swinging 60s cover art, but ignoring the social and cultural snobbery, it's a powerful cover.

5000 Spirits... is a brilliant album too, of its time but also timeless. Just because an album is most definitely from a specific era, does not mean it doesn't retain its full power, its ability to entertain and baffle in equal measure. This album is not a "safe" place musically; it's totally unpredictable, often challenging to an unsuspecting pair of ears, but purely beautiful at the same time.

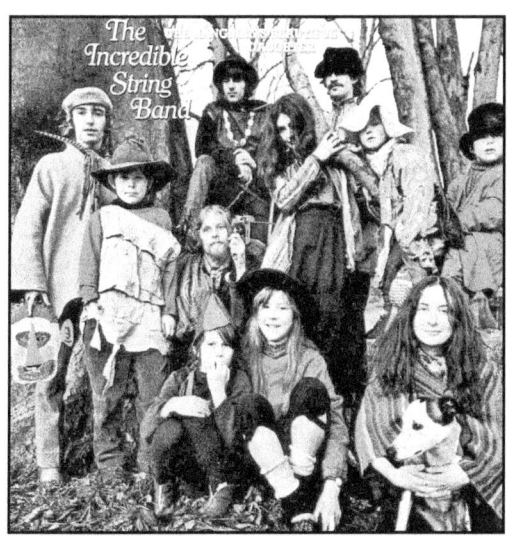

The Hangman's Beautiful Daughter (1968)

*"To me, the String Band albums are very much born a clash
and reconciliation of tastes."*
- Mike Heron, Beat Instrumental

If there is one year that can be named as the ISB's pinnacle then it is definitely 1968. For starters they were at their most popular amidst the flower power bloom, adored and worshipped by their many followers worldwide. In this year alone they cut what many regard as their two seminal LPS, The Hangman's Beautiful Daughter and Wee Tam and the Big Huge. Both were successful albums, which tells you just how open pop buyers were back in the sixties.

Before the album's release, the ISB had made a giant leap when they were invited to play the 1967 Newport Folk festival. They went down a storm and Boyd recalls Leonard Cohen and Joni Mitchell being completely blown away by them, in awe of their unconventional and totally original style. 5000 Spirits and the songs of that era had clearly established them as key players in folk, but Hangman's Beautiful Daughter moved them along even further. The album saw the lyrical themes and musical direction become even more outlandish, imaginative, dreamlike and certainly more experimental, yet not recklessly so.

On the way back from a US trip in 1967, Mike and Robin had nipped into Elektra's New York City headquarters and "helped themselves" to some new LPs from Nonesuch International Series, a company releasing Eastern music in the Western world. Under Mike and Robin's arms that day were records of Japanese kabuki theatre, popular Greek music, and even a compilation album of guitarists from the Bahamas. Clearly, it was about taking in as much as possible and not just whatever was entering the living room on TV's Top of the Pops. Mike and Robin may have not invented the sounds they were making, but they were clever and inquisitive enough to combine sounds from all over the world and put them on to one record in an original way.

By now, Heron and Williamson's then girlfriends were turning out to be full time members. As well as Licorice showing real promise musically, Mike's girlfriend Rose Simpson was also taking on a number of instruments, learning as she went along but becoming a fairly decent bass player in her own right. It was Williamson who originally had a liaison with Rose, but after a gig in York she had got out of Robin's bed and into Mike's sleeping bag, beginning their famous romance. "Rose was and still is as bright, cheerful and outgoing as Licorice was dour and secretive," Boyd wrote in his autobiography. "Her laughter is as hearty as Mike's and the pair were a delight to be around."

But how did she get involved in the music? Boyd claimed once that Heron was feeling outnumbered, and so wanted to get his girlfriend in on the act too, but how true this is we'll never know. In Boyd's recollection he threw a bass in her hand and said "learn that!" It needs to be said that the thought of Mike throwing anything at anyone is a little hard to swallow. But Rose took the rough with the smooth, mastering her instrument in her own way, "bumbling along" as she put it. "Smile and say hello. If someone gives you something, hit it or ring it... just go along with it really."

Boyd recalled that he had initially thought Licorice was "just a temporary passenger. How wrong could I be? She had a sweet small face marred by a chipped front tooth she never sought to repair. Her dark hair hung down lank and uncombed. She wore wool skirts so carelessly that her aversion to underwear became obvious... she rarely spoke and when she did it was in a squeaky voice with the thickest of Scots accents... Robin was under her thumb. She could alter the direction of a discussion with a steely glance or a murmur."

This aside, recording on the album would commence with four permanent band members. There were also some unexpected guest appearances too. Judy Dyble, she of Fairport Convention and later Trader Horne, was present at the recording of the album.

"I didn't 'work' on the album as such," she told me. "ISB happened to be in the studio when Fairport were there waiting to do a session and they needed backing vocals on The Minotaur's Song. So we were all (Fairport) drafted in to be the scratch choir. Just one of those 'being in the right place at the right time' things again."

Recording techniques in the music industry had started to shift by 1968 and the ISB moved along with the advancements. No longer was it a case of crowding round one microphone in the centre of the room and making sure you were heard. It had all become much sophisticated.

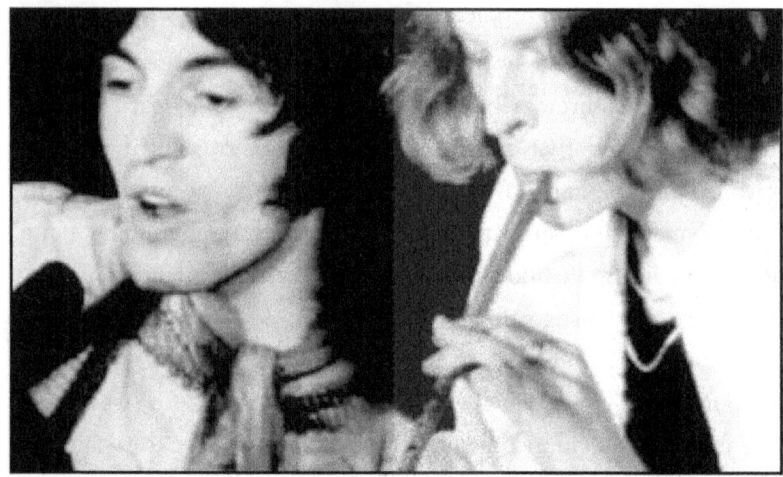

"By the time we got to the second record," Robin said. "We were jumping tracks, and by the time we got to the third... it came to be like painting. And that was a wonderful opening of a door. I always loved the idea you could sort of put something on and rub it out and try something else. That really began to be born in the studio. It was things you could do, we'd then try to re-create live."

At the time, Boyd thought it was the best produced album he had been involved with so far and for me, The Hangman's Beautiful Daughter has the best sound for an ISB album, and the finest opening tracks of all their records. Starting like a hazy sweet dream, Williamson brings us into the colourful proceedings with Koeeoaddi There, his mysterious and moving portrait of a childhood that may or may not be real (either way seems beside the point anyway). Memories mirror your own throughout the song, with Williamson's imagery so vivid it could be coming directly from a legendary poet's childhood diary. Still, the melodies visit the listener briefly, make you smile and reflect, before they disappear as mysteriously and quickly as they appeared, being swiftly replaced by an even sweeter melody in an instant. For one song under five minutes to have this many moods, styles, tunes and rich ideas in it is very rare indeed and lovely turns of phrase like "setting your foot where the sand is untrodden" seem just as musical as the Noah's Ark of instruments populating the song itself. The baker's stubbly grin, the bear Mrs Thompson gave him, the woman with the bulldozer, Bridgette and the people upstairs, skating on happy valley pond... the lines are endless and scenarios float and fly by as the song reaches its climax, with the rapid riddle of "earth water fire and death...."

Williamson later remembered the track in an interview.

"If you answer the riddle you'll never begin; there's no answer to the riddle, but the whole song itself was a dream from start to finish, the dream I had put to music, so it has the same logic that the dream has, which is not much logic. There are bits and pieces about early memories in Edinburgh and so forth, but it's a collage song with bits of this dream, bits of early childhood, and it's basically the fact that I consider that life is pretty much an unanswerable riddle, with not really much of an answer to it some of the times. I think that's its magic. Anyway that's what that song says."

The album continues its daydreaming with the surreal pre-Monty Python mock jollity of The Minotaur's Song, where medieval England and the poshest choir imaginable assault the senses from every angle. Knowing the ISB had such a great sense of absurd humour gives the album another shade of character. It also showcases another recurring style throughout the band's records; vaudeville, and even hints of camp, sing-along British musical hall. As well as folk and world music, they were also taking in mainstream British traditions too; ones from decades earlier, centuries even. Nothing was out of bounds for the ISB collage.

"Certainly, the children have seen them," must surely be one of the most chilling opening lines to a song ever, and once again Williamson brings us more fantastically haunting imagery in Witches Hat, which also features the unforgettable line "next week a monkey is coming to stay." Musically the song conjures images of children playing in the high grass, chasing fairies, and the mad flute section that clashes with the guitar melody suggests more magic. It's childhood again, rich and wondrously exploring the wild, seemingly endless summer days we had as kids, our fearless adventures and plots and schemes. Or of course, it could all be another dream. Memories, after all, the further they reach back, can often have the same mental atmosphere as a long lost dream, with indescribable scents and hazy landscapes you barely recall. What is a dream and what is reality? Perhaps this theory best sums up the moods of your average ISB album, the muddled results of moulding together two states of consciousness.

The first Heron penned song here is the epic A Very Cellular Song, at times a heavenly hymn, a celebration of the lord and life itself, while drifting in and out of discordant oddity just as much as it delights in its own divinity. "All it was, was a trip," Heron said of the song and its inspiration. "And that was the music I was listening to, that and interspersed with Radio 4, bits of plays, people talking to each other, and I happened to be listening to the Pinder Family before I started." The Pinder Family had sung We Bid You Goodnight, a section of which is included in the song. Heron had also admitted he had written the song whilst on acid. "It wasn't personal though," he said. "I was writing a song for the world while on acid." He also once called it a "diary of a trip."

"The classic track is A Very Cellular Song," Boyd later said. "Which is almost like a suite of songs, in which he brings hymns and oriental this and medieval that. Cellular images were very prevalent in discussions about psychedelia, the idea that when you were high you could look at your hands and see the cellular construction of your flesh and you could actually break down and perceive what was going on under this calm exterior of your skin."

When one of the girls is heard whispering "Amoebas are very small", it brings in my personal favourite section of the song, a gently sung verse by the Amoeba himself. "If an Amoeba was feeling a bit lonely they would just split down the middle," Mike later chuckled. "They wouldn't have to bother with sex or anything like that. That's the implication of that particular bit." And the song slithers and squelches on, eventually culminating in Mike's lovely blessing at the end.

The scale of this 13 minute epic is almost like a full album in itself, yet it only merely finishes off side A and there are still 6 tracks to go, 2 more penned by Heron and 4 more Williamson cuts. Still, I personally feel these four opening tracks are among the very finest the ISB ever committed to vinyl.

Of the album's title, Heron stated at the time, "The hangman is death and the beautiful daughter is what comes after. Or you might say that the hangman is the past twenty years of our life and the beautiful daughter is now, what we are able to do after all these years. Or you can make up your own meaning - your interpretation is probably just as good as ours."

With Robin stating the whole album was meant to be like a dream, you find yourself going along with that definition much easier. Sure, an album doesn't necessarily need a theme for you to enjoy it, but to know the occasional lunacy and the constantly changing themes, ideas and stories are tied together with a loose concept, certainly gives the album a well rounded balance.

Such matters didn't seem to enter the public's minds at the time the record was released though. In March of 1968 it was released and peaked at Number 5 in the UK charts, but only climbed into the top 200 in the US on their Billboard chart. It didn't help matters that America's biggest music magazine, Rolling Stone gave the album a cold review. Admitting the Minotaur's Song was a good track, they added "Heron and Williamson are superb musicians, on this album they apparently forgot it... they didn't know where they were going." However DJ John Peel championed the band and played this album heavily on his influential show, ensuring UK success.

The wonderful album cover shot of the band, with the girls and the gathered children, deserves more than a passing note. It was Christmas 1967 and the four ISB members were staying with their friend Mary Stewart in Baltimore. The children in the image are Mary's and the chaps in the back are two other friends Roger Stewart and Nicky Walton. A great article published in the 90s tracked down some of the children. One was Robbie, three years old on the cover, who recalled the photo "shoot."

"I have brief memories of that picture being taken, walking through the woods, dressed all funny, but that's it. A lot of things were a big game at the time. It didn't mean anything to me to be on the cover as such, but I grew up loving music, whereas everyone else at school was into football." Such naivety from one of its cover stars fitted the music within its iconic sleeve perfectly. The reverse side of the album, often used as the cover in some editions, is a rather striking image of Mike and Robin in full eccentric garb set against a bright blue sky. Either picture is cover worthy, epitomising the ISB in their 60s tripped out prime.

So many retrospective reviews of the ISB albums looking at this period dive straight into the drug connection, the thought of taking LSD then putting the album on the turntable and feeling your mind expand. Of course it is nonsense. Heron and Williamson never set out to make music that could only be enjoyable while under the influence of heavy drugs, even if they most certainly were on acid when they wrote it. In many ways, The Hangman's Beautiful Daughter and some of the other records are a drug in themselves. For the inquisitive forward thinking music fan, the album shows that anything is possible in music, that there need not be any boundaries. As a musician I really admire that outlook and can enjoy it with a cup of tea and a Hobnob, rather than with a heavy helping of acid. Maybe I'll try both at once one day...

Of course the ISB, it can be said are the perfect musician's band. A lot of people can write a song, a 3 minute ditty especially, with the standard chords and the expected structure. It's fun doing so in fact. But when listening to the ISB as a musician, there most certainly could be an amount of envy brewed up when listening closely. There is no traditional form at all; the lyrics are so imaginative you can't imagine where they have come from. If you tried to do a song in their style, you would end up sounding like some escaped loony. There is something to be said for individuality that can not be replicated.

The flavours injected by the girls also need to be noted. Boyd, although being impressed and touched by the natural progression Rose experienced on the bass, noted that he felt their involvement marked the beginning of the "decline" in quality with the ISB's releases. In my opinion he could not be more wrong. Some of their finest work lay before them.

The Hangman's Beautiful Daughter is still probably their most influential album. There is the famous quote of Robert Plant, where he said Led Zeppelin took Hangman's Beautiful Daughter and simply followed the instructions. But there are more moments where Zeppelin and ISB cross over. Plant mentioned them in Q magazine in 1993.

"We'd always had their records, but we were playing at the Usher Hall in Edinburgh and Robin and Mike came along, and found that, despite the bamboozle and the noise of Led Zeppelin, there was some kind of Celtic folk music beating in the middle of it too, something tangible despite the macho gestures. And I suppose we started a sort of mutual appreciation society. I love their storytelling and their capacity to charm with lines like 'I hear that the Emperor of China used to wear iron shoes with ease.' Up until then I'd been more concerned with why Howling Wolf would climb to the top of the curtains and slide down them at the age of 56 and weighing 200 pounds while playing harmonica. The Incredible String Band was tales from another place altogether. I thought their whole communion of audience and musical troupe was absolutely wonderful. However, somehow or other The Prince of Darkness drew me closer and closer to Alice Cooper and the ridiculousness of rock culture and I kept looking behind wistfully as I jumped on the starship and went off to commit more carnal atrocities. The one thing we always wanted to do in Led Zeppelin was to finish off the show with the String Band's A Very Cellular Song, the bit that goes 'I was walking in Jerusalem just like John. Goodnight, goodnight.' But Bonham, bless him, said something very like Fuck Off!"

You wouldn't listen to Zeppelin and immediately think of the Increds, but influences do not always come out in the most obvious way. While often subconscious, they clearly sometimes externalise as a straight homage. For instance, Zeppelin's classic movie The Song Remains the Same is very reminiscent of the ISB's own film, Be Glad

For the Song Has No Ending, both in title and content. They even filmed it in Wales and made it more than a little mystical to say the least. Plant has always shown his fondness for the band; befriending Rose in the 90s for instance, and asking Robin to play support for his and Page's MTV Unplugged appearance, which unfortunately never happened. Stairway to Heaven, with its flute lines and complex weaving chords, owes more than a note or two to the ISB.

Its influence aside, the album is simply a gem and you can never tire of its invention, the eclectic collage of sounds within it. It's maybe a good place to start when approaching the band's discography.

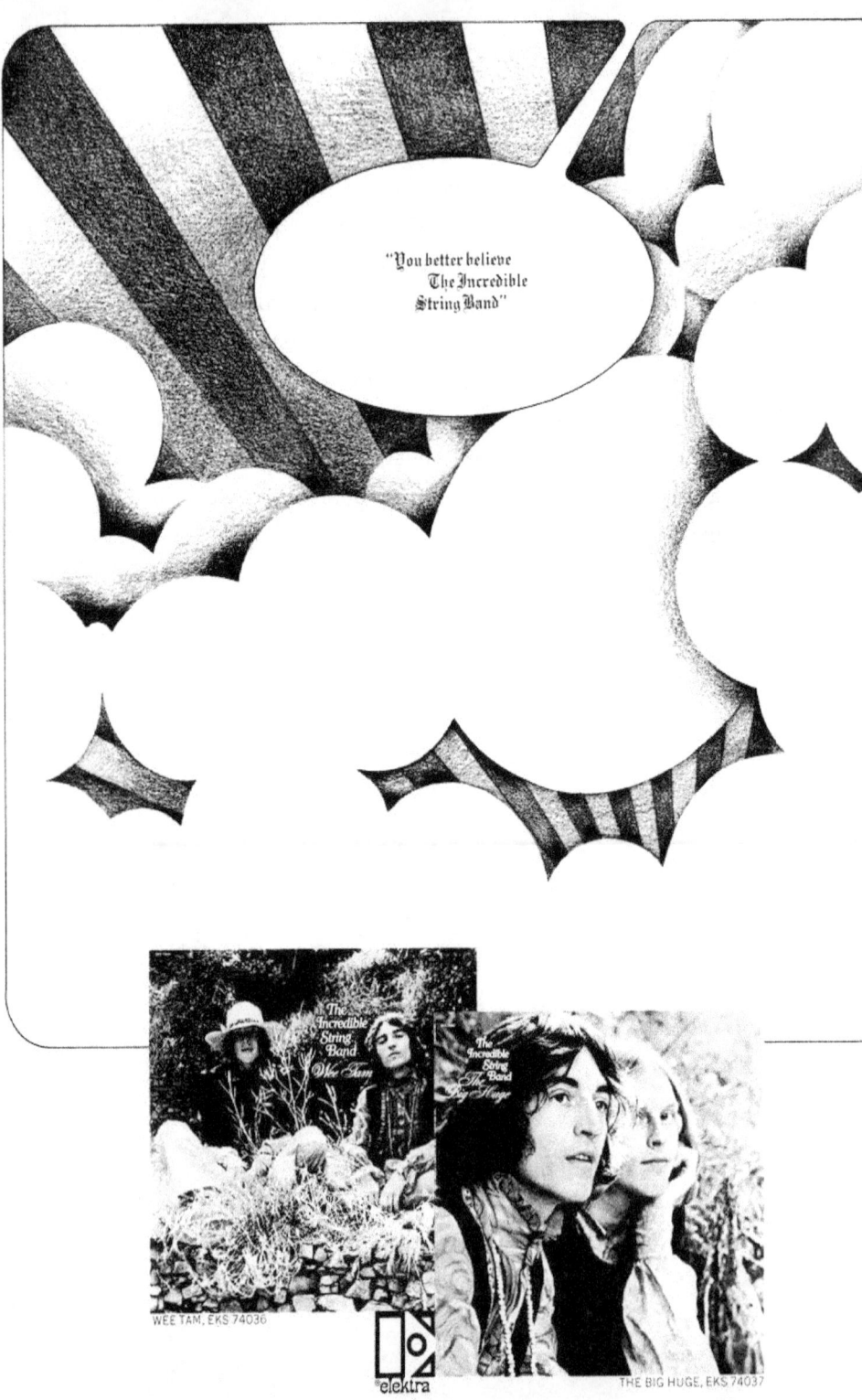

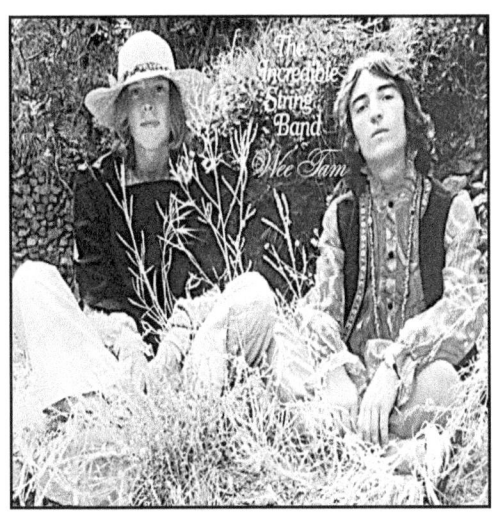

Wee Tam and
the Big Huge
(1968)

"I saw a man with a huge big dog, and we knew somebody called Wee Tam, in Edinburgh. It seemed like it was a good idea in terms of one person looking up at the stars - Wee Tam and the Big Huge, just like the vastness of the universe."

— Robin Williamson.

Apart from Hangman's Beautiful Daughter, Wee Tam and the Big Huge is probably the Incredible String Band's most lauded and acclaimed album and it certainly is among their most imaginative. Curiously released both as a double album in the UK and two separate LPs in America, this may have created commercial confusion. But with complications aside, buyers must have been happy with their purchase, for this record features some of Mike and Robin's finest ever songs.

In 1968 it was onward and upward for the band. Out of the clubs and into the major venues, the ISB took on two of the country's most prestigious venues, the Royal Festival Hall and The Royal Albert Hall.

In America the ISB were going down a storm too. They played the Fillmore West in San Francisco and went on to play Fillmore East in New York, both legendary stints for the band.

"The audiences in America were fantastically patient in 67, 68, 69," Robin said. "A good example of that is, we were supposed to do a gig once in the Fillmore West. The equipment had been loaded off the plane without us knowing it from the freight in Canada somewhere, because we were coming from Canada. So we arrived in San Francisco with no instruments. And we were supposed to play. All I had was a three string North African instrument called a Gimbri and a bow. So the audience sat for 3 hours going 'hmmm' which I played along with. I actually got this on tape."

After their Fillmore East performance, they met David Simons, who got the band interested in Scientology, an incident that instantly sparked controversy within their die hard fan base. Admirers have noted the gradual decline in their material from here on after, but one can only speculate if Scientology had any effect on their output whatsoever. After all, the band went on to make 8 more records after Wee Tam. Ironically, given his obvious and well documented contempt for the band's involvement with Scientology, it was Boyd himself who introduced the band to his old friend Simons.

But before any complications entered the band's creative and personal world, Wee Tam and the Big Huge had the boys at their finest. Released in November of 1968, the same year The Hangman's

Beautiful Daughter had established them as pop's new bizarre troubadours, they were now delivering two LPS of pure eccentric gold.

Job's Tears is a classic opening track, with Williamson's wild vocals at first seeming aimless in melody, searching for the right note while writhing above the conventions we expect and twisting his voice into the most unlikely areas. The song culminates in the blissful "all will be one" section, with gorgeous backing vocals by Licorice behind Wiliamson's nursery rhyme utopia. "I won't need to miss you when we're there," he says, "all will be one."

The whole surreal feel of Puppies, with its spiky sitar, sliding guitar parts and acoustic drive naturally bring us into what seems like the more grounded Heron territory. However, grounded it most certainly is not. Mike has often spoken of how he wrote this track while tripping on acid. There is a blissful feel to this song however, with Heron's harmonised voices playing against each other brilliantly in the mix. "That's pretty much a solo effort," Mike later said. "That's actually just me in the studio I think. It was a bit trippy. We were over in America and Joe knew some girl who had a dog, and it was having puppies at the time. It was a husky type dog, not really a pet. And they were leaping off into the woods and bringing odd stuff back. So that's how that came about. And the way I did it was just in the studio with lots of multi tracking and a weird echoey thing, which has a bit to do with LSD."

Things are given a slight intermission with the quick but nice Yellow Snake, a soothing, introverted sitar led piece written and sung by Williamson, with Heron's wonderful sitar part floating around you like a jesting spirit (especially when listening on headphones). With so many of their songs being very long, it's refreshing for one to be a mere 2 minutes in length; in this case though it's just too short.

Log Cabin Home in the Sky proves that Heron was no slouch in the songwriting department, even in an era when Robin was shining at his brightest. Heron recently noted that he felt eclipsed by Williamson around this period, but there is no reason to believe that Robin's songs are any better than Mike's. Robin's, by 1968, have taken on an even stronger and more spiritual poetic power, and Heron's remain more straight forward, often drifting slightly into the unknown, but remaining much easier to get into on first listen. Log Cabin Home in the Sky is a joyful jig with some lovely guitar and violin interplay, and a lyric melody that is impossible to shake off. A genuine classic, Heron plays it live to this day.

When you listen to the album, you hear the shifts in tone, but not for one second do you see Heron and Williamson's roles clashing with one another. However, a live review from 1969 printed in Rolling Stone was more than comfortable in comparing the two men's talents. "I assumed it was Heron who led the band along," they wrote. "Clearly though, Williamson leads. It isn't an equal partnership. Heron was far from being peripheral but he seemed content to take a back seat." Bear in mind they had seen a live show (in York), a medium where Robin was much more wild and extroverted, leaping from instrument to instrument like some hyperactive pixie, while Heron, as he is today, was always the solid reliable singer/guitarist. Both have charm in equal measure in my view.

You Get Brighter heads off side 2, another cheerful Heron number with medieval harpsichord lines caterpillaring up and down the scales. When it comes to The Half Remarkable Question however, Williamson enters his own league. That simple melody, over the chugging acoustic strum, is instantly burrowed into the mind and refuses to leave. Robin's voice, stoned and dreamy, brings you into his universe with an

ease, while Heron scatters elegantly throughout with subtle sitar lines. The well known ISB rule, that Williamson should allow Heron to leave his mark on his song, and vice versa, is here at its most successful.

"In the early days, Mike and Robin used to tear each other's songs to bits," Joe Boyd recalled. "They would argue a lot and be intent on imposing their own stamp on each other's songs. If a Robin song was to enter the ISB repertoire, by God Mike was going to make people remember the sitar part. There was a very healthy level of competitiveness..."

"The freckles of rain are telling me so." Does one even need to know what this song is about? To dissect its beauty, after all, may just be to wreck its sheer perfection. As Robin once noted, the ISB songs are best left to the imagination of the listener. I think it best to sometimes take a step back and merely enjoy the rhythm and flow of Robin's words, pulling out the strings of imagery yourself.

Air is another fine Heron song, now something of a classic to the ISB fans. It starts with that familiar organ/flute tune, before the surreal muted choir of hums begins, conjuring images of strange lazy songbirds slumbering in trees. Mike's vocal comes in much deeper than usual, uttering mysterious lyrics like "you kiss my blood" which makes the song a little darker than it immediately seems to be. It has a real unspoilt purity about it though, and you can just picture the feral creatures of the wild circling the band as they sing. It's incredibly beautiful stuff. Close your eyes and listen to Heron's intimate whispering vocal (almost like a relaxation tape), the sounds approaching you from either side and the masterful production by Boyd. Definitely a stand out from the whole set.

Williamson's childlike Ducks on a Pond follows with its charming simplicity. "Ducks on a pond, very pretty swimming round" is most definitely a twee lyric, but the song develops into a more magical and mysterious fairytale, with whistling and tripped out Lewis Carroll-esque lyrics running along to a perfect collection of Williamson melodies.

The second record, entitled The Big Huge begins with Maya, one of Williamson's classic 10 minute psych folk masterpieces. It transforms back and forth between a contemplative acoustic monologue and a bongo driven jangle fest complete with signature sitar playing from Mike. Williamson's words cast a spell once again, their curiosity only enhancing the wonderment of the arrangement.

He continues to mostly dominate the rest of the set, Lordly Nightshade being a particular stand out for me. For opening lines, can you get any better than "Captured by Hitler with Oliver Twist in the tower?" Such daringly unconventional words, ones not even buried within the song, but in fact being the opening line, show an admirable sense of distorting the conventions of music. It's clearly a strange lyric, perhaps as strange as one can get in this song format, yet it doesn't sound the least bit contrived or pretentious (nor does any of their work for that matter). It's perhaps the most enchanting, spaced out track on the album, yet its slight air of drug influence never takes too much of a sinister turn, thanks to the snare drum march and sweet flute lines. It's still totally innocent and the words, though maybe impossible to decipher (even if you asked Williamson what they meant) are best taken once again as "jazz poetry", a chain of words that sound so sweet together, even though they often can appear to be a little disturbing. Ending with "all on a summer's day" and the sound of wind chimes though soothes away anything that could have been taken as too "heavy." Once again, the ISB's clear drug influence is understated, accompanied by gorgeously inventive and colourful sounds fit for an idyllic childhood.

Opening side B of The Big Huge is a Heron gem, Cousin Caterpillar. Such delicate and dazzling lyrics, unblemished as they are clash brilliantly with Williamson's Celtic, jaunty, jagged Iron Stone, a song which has forever been cemented and preserved thanks to its inclusion in their classic film Be Glad for the Song Has No Ending. The awkward, almost impossible chords and the way they float and shift with ease, boggles the mind. Try and imitate a song like this and you will come out looking like a fool.

The album climaxes with a definite Williamson classic, The Circle is Unbroken. Beginning with a lovely penny whistle line by Robin, the song boasts some superb streaming harp notes, a true feeling of old and some wonderful Williamson words. It's hard to think of a more soothing and perfect way to finish an album of often eccentric variety.

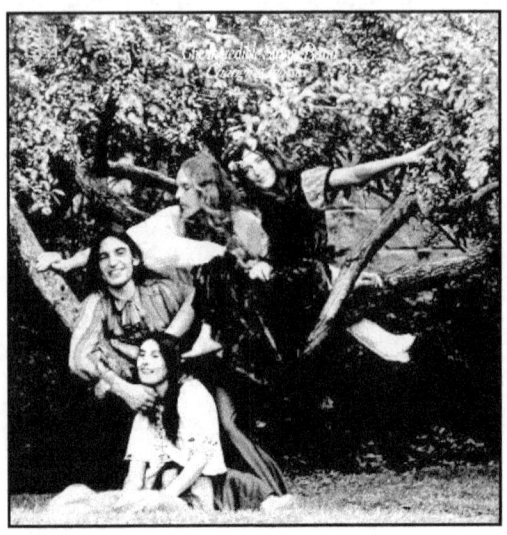

Changing Horses
(1969)

By 1969, the ISB were broadening their creative ideas and developing their skills in other areas. Most of the band were now living together in a farmhouse near Newport, Wales, very much the hippy Communal life style. This era was captured in the wonderful BBC film Be Glad for the Song Has No Ending, a half documentary, half creative film project that would later gain a cult following on VHS and DVD. The first half follows the band to gigs, asks them a few questions on their creative process, and even shows Robin visiting his luthier. The second half of the film is either totally mad or totally brilliant, me opting for the latter, consisting of a short film entitled The Pirate and the Crystal Ball. The brilliantly imaginative fable was accompanied by some fantastically creative music especially conducted and produced for the album, once again by Joe Boyd, the whole of which was released in 1971 on record as simply Be Glad for the Song Has No Ending. Williamson has often expressed dissatisfaction with the results of the film itself, claiming he could have done a few things better if he'd had more time to figure them out, but that would have only taken away the beautiful naivety of it all. It's a moment in time forever preserved, imperfect and wonderful forever.

It was in 1969 of course that the band travelled to the USA and famously played Woodstock Festival, at first described by Boyd to the band as a "little up-state festival." Largely seen as a missed opportunity for the ISB, they refused to play in the rain on the opening night, which was especially for the folk and acoustic bands, and instead played their set the following night, going on after, of all people, the energetic rockers Canned Heat. Everybody was stoned beyond belief by then and just wanted to groove along to some heavy rock. The ISB didn't quite fit the bill.

"That was through people who knew Joe," Mike later said. "We'd done this show in New York the night before and the organisers were keen to have us on. A helicopter took us to the site and I recall all these people looking like ants trapped in a sea of mud. I don't know what we were doing then but we played and left again." In typical charming, forgetful Heron form, he concluded with "I think the girls were with us then."

On Radio 2 in 2013, Heron recalled coming into Woodstock in a chopper with Ravi Shankar, who asked the pilot "what is that crop?" It was then of course he realised the "crop" in question was the mass Woodstock hippy crowd, gathered throughout the field. As the helicopter was a military one, it had an open side. As the pilot tipped the chopper over so Ravi could get a closer look, the passengers had to hold on for dear life or they would have gone flying out of the chopper. "We were completely terrified, but Ravi was more terrified, which gave us some kind of comfort," Mike chuckled.

Boyd desperately tried to get them on the stage, but they refused and gave their slot to Melanie, who went on to give an iconic and unforgettable performance.

"It was Joe Boyd's Greatest Mistake," the man himself later confessed. "If I could do it all over again I would put them on in the rain. They would have triumphed like Melanie. They would have been in the movie, and everyone who was in the movie had a huge break. Who knows what would have happened?"

Heron admits their performance wasn't great (he also commented that Boyd can often become "unbearable" when recounting these tales) and that they were not quite suitable for such a massive rock oriented shindig, while Rose later said they should have stopped moaning about the rain and just got on stage, maybe played some of the older non-electric numbers. Either way, it can't change a thing now. The ISB story may have been different had they played the acoustic night, but then it might also have been the same. After all, Ten Years After played a storming set at Woodstock and it's definitely the main thing people remember them for, cementing them firmly into that one single event forever. At least the Increds will always exist in their own weird little universe, and if someone does discover and approach them with curiosity, it is for their music rather than for their brief appearance on one special night in time. Besides, Heron still got to watch Hendrix play the Star Spangled Banner from the side of the stage. "It was absolutely startling," he said. "Watching him do that, it felt like the world was about to change, that nothing would be the same again."

In November, their next LP Changing Horses was released. Although seen as a disappointment to fans upon release, it's strangely my personal favourite of their albums. It's a brilliantly weird set, plain surreal at time, climaxing of course with the huge, often scary, hypnotic, and ever changing masterpiece Creation, the arrival of all that exists squashed into a beautiful quarter of an hour. It's one of those songs that goes on and on for so long that you just get lost in it, hypnotised by the repetitive chords, swept away by the endless chant and Williamson's beautiful delivery of the words. For me, it's possibly their best moment and even though it may be over 15 minutes, I always want to put it straight back on as soon as it has finished.

The album has two epic tracks in fact, Heron's exuberant White Bird and Williamson's afore mentioned Creation. Asked by Mark Radcliffe in 2013 if it was a conscious decision to have 2 epic 15 minute tracks on the album, Heron answered "Yes. Nearly all the albums came out of shows, so during the Creation thing I said kind of 'play,' in the odd kind of hippy play thing and it came on the record that way."

It was prior to Changing Horses that the band became interested in Scientology of course. In one interview, Williamson commented on the liberated and indirect aspect of their epics, in particular his own Creation, and although he has confessed that Scientology maybe had an effect on his songwriting (perhaps sometimes influencing a more direct intention in song), he also claimed he kept it separate from his music, holding it firmly and solely as a belief.

"It was very sort of loose," he said of the song. "Creation is one of the least direct songs that I've ever written. It's very rambling indeed. Based around seven days of creation and a whole bunch of other ideas thrown in there. It lasts fifteen minutes. So it couldn't be called exactly direct, so in the end all these inferences and trying to relate things to times they don't really pan out that well, because I've always found that things happening in my life don't necessarily reflect that directly in the music, although Scientology was very helpful to me as a philosophy. I wouldn't try to trace its influence in my music, because my music has always pursued pretty much its own course, you know, almost independent of my life."

In 1971, Mike spoke of his new found discovery of Scientology to Beat Instrumental. "I guess it was in the middle of making Wee Tam that we got into it. Each one of us became involved at separate times. At first we thought it would be a direct influence on our song writing but later we came to realise that it was precisely in this area that we had the most highly developed perception already. It was when we put our guitars down and came to make a cup of tea or talk to a chick that we were goofy and got depressed. So it is in these areas that we developed most easily. Particularly in communication and just experiencing life. We had become too tied to our guitar strings. So the way in which our writing and composing has really been affected is by putting our lives in order. We now have the ability to set ourselves to something we want to do and really do it. It would have been impossible for us to get a pantomime together in druggie days. Just impossible."

Of course, Scientology becomes irrelevant when simply enjoying their albums. In many ways the music of ISB perfectly sums up the endless creative possibilities that some artists were lucky enough to have in the 1960s recording industry, as well as the naivety, the freedom and sense of world changing. This music may be very reflective of its era, but it is not strictly of its time. One can look back to their music and almost be envious of their limitless abilities. Here they were, signed to a major label, for a brief time a contending album chart act, both completely avant-garde and totally approachable. Only in the 1960s could a band this imaginative be a part of mainstream pop music. It's fairly well known that The Beatles were enjoying their music before going in to make Sgt Pepper, and that Paul McCartney said 5000 Spirits... was one of his favourite albums of 1967. And you can believe it too. ISB's playfulness is at times close to out and out bonkers avant-garde experimentation, often bordering on such an unusual territory that it might not be listenable, but only for around 10 seconds, and they always pull it back again in time for you to get your head together. The Beatles and The Rolling Stones toyed with these elements but remained with their feet more firmly on the ground, always more melodic and conscious of their commercial appeal and the risks of going too far out. Perhaps The Beatles, in some strange way, were slightly envious that bands like the ISB could be as free as they liked, for they didn't have that pressure of the whole world dissecting every chord and syllable.

The album starts with a cheery number, Big Ted, a shuffle that morphs into a boogie woogie piano rock out. It's full of an innocent humour, almost like a children's song. It is in fact an ode to a dead pig, a large dead pig at that, which has now departed this world and entered the great pig sty in the sky. Its lyrics were born out of Heron's views of the hippy communal lifestyle some of the band were now aiming for. "He (Robin) wanted a commune life, but I didn't fancy living in a farmhouse and fighting over the kitchen, that kind of thing. They were into macrobiotics and chocolate was banned. They would live on brown rice, which was where the song

Big Ted comes in. They had their whole winter's supply of rice stored, and the pig got in and ate it all."

Dust Be Diamonds is Robin's brilliant kazoo splattered hippy odyssey, with chirpy backing vocals from Mike and the girls together. Its simple approach tells us that all is what we make of it, that it's all alright if you really want it to be. As the album progresses, you get the sense there is more of a childish element to the music. Of course, they had been playful before and their use of instruments was often in good humour, but Changing Horses could be their most spontaneous and innocent set of songs in all, definitely closer to the modern idea of hippy music than much of their other work. The fact there were no drugs on board the ISB train any more may have had something to do with it.

Sleepers Awake is a notable addition to the set in that it contains no actual music. Heron takes the formative vocal part on his beautiful hymn, with Robin closely following with a perfectly distanced harmony. The girls though shine brightest and if Licorice's cries reached any higher they'd be right in the heavens that Mike sings of being so near. No wacky instrumentation needed, the glorious words speak for themselves.

Mr and Mrs is another Robin gem, and he recalled its inspiration years later, and how maybe the free form element of his writing was beginning to change.

"Well it was talking about the middle classes wasn't it?" he said. "The 50's and the middle classes and it was just a picture of that really. All those images were carefully chosen; that wasn't a spontaneous kind of work, by that time I was getting into construct things almost like verbal sculptures. There were two different layers. Early on in particular I tried to write in a very free flowing way, but later on, influenced by Dylan Thomas I tried to use words in a very concrete way and pick words very carefully, and sometimes work on a song for quite a long time."

The fact that the band had now converted fully to Scientology and given up taking any drugs is quite apparent in the sounds on the LP. Changing Horses almost has a holy essence, some purity, and is lacking much of the druggier elements of their earlier works. Perhaps this is why the album is not as highly rated by ISB fans, the fact it isn't characteristic of the popular idea of the ISB. Personally I find it a much more honest statement if anything, a brilliant transitional record bridging the gap for the band, from the idealistic 60s towards the fresh and new landscape of the 1970s.

In 1968, Mike and Robin, along with Boyd, had visited the Maharishi Mahesh Yogi, prior to him spending time with The Beatles in India. Although they had studied Buddhism, they were also very interested in the practice of meditation and were keen to get his advice on the matter. The Yogi however was not interested in discussing techniques, saying that it was only worth anything when the Yogi himself had given out the mantra... for a fee of course. They left feeling slightly cheated by the Yogi, who came across as more of a businessman rather than a guru. "It puzzled me that they left so disillusioned," Boyd dryly noted. "Yet a few months later they were ready to sign on for something far more businesslike and formularised."

That being Scientology of course...

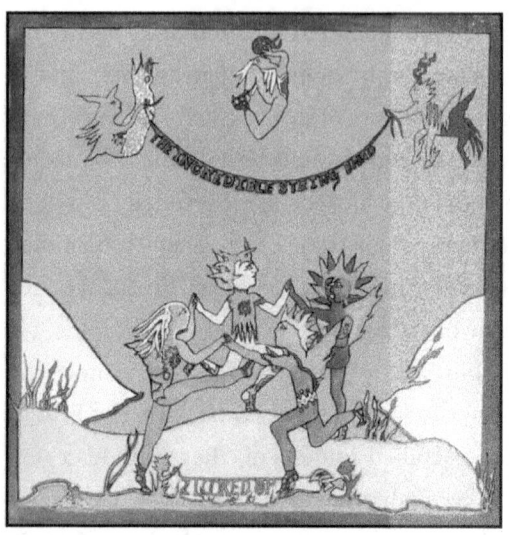

I Looked Up
(1970)

Leaving the naïve, dreamy landscape of the 1960s behind, it was inevitable that things would change for the ISB, as they did for everyone, musically or otherwise. Playing Woodstock, epitomising the flower power era, selling tons of records and selling out concert halls the world over, the band had clearly succeeded in every area a band can, but it was clear that the new decade would bring in new styles, trends and fashions. The Vietnam War raged on of course, prog rock and the early stages of heavy metal were already emerging. Ten minute guitar wig outs, twiddly keyboard runs and ridiculously outsized stadium gigs were on the way. The ISB, those four happy smiling figures with a gallery of musical instruments from all over the globe, singing of farm yards, hedgehogs and caterpillars, honest and innocent songs of hope; just where would they fit into all this?

Glen Row, near Innerleithen on the Scottish borders, is where the ISB chose their next home base. Once again living close together in a row of cottages, the ISB dynamic had altered somewhat. Mike and Rose had parted ways as a couple, as had Robin and Licorice, and the music was beginning to alter. I Looked Up is perhaps the last album that sounds distinctively like classic, trademark ISB. Admittedly recorded as a quickie according to Williamson, the band were already devoted to their next project, the elaborate stage show U.

I Looked Up opens with Black Jack Davy, a standard yet enjoyable violin led piece penned by Heron. Cheery and upbeat, it makes for a great introduction into the set. It is on I Looked Up that Mike leads the way in the songwriting field for the first time, with him writing all but two tracks, the others being Robin's Pictures in a Mirror and When You Find Out Who You Are.

The second track is Letter, which the band famously played at Woodstock, with the off beat opening riff leading into a sleepy Mike melody. It's a nice if slightly forgettable number. The same cannot be said for Heron's This Moment, to this day one of the most treasured songs in their catalogue. With its flowing chord progression, catchy melody and blissful backing vocals, this song stands up to the best ISB work. The lovely lyrics tell of sweet moments with a lover and the possibilities of a love that exists in the hands of fate. The Robin and Likky middle 8 parts are beautiful, as Heron calls out in bliss in the background. Then there are the trademark slices of ISB humour, the glorious "oh gosh and golly, no" parts, and the occasional giggles from the girls, showing the band never took themselves too seriously.

It's one song that I feel perfectly sums up the whole 60s ethic, those lost ideals of peace and love, a time when it seemed possible for mankind to reach an eventual sort of Utopia. Of course, it was not to be. After all, the 60s were now over and the ISB's glorious sound no longer reflected the increasingly harsh and turbulent times. It could be the distinct point where the ISB world alters, this one iconic number, still clinging on to the loved up atmosphere of the previous decade.

The record as a whole though does have that "quickie" feel about it, even though it often reaches magical highs. I'm not sure just how much thought and passion went into every track, especially from Robin's end, as he feels somewhat absent from proceedings. It does have some wonderful stuff on it, but it feels more like a stepping stone towards something else, which of course it is! Boyd's handling of the songs doesn't seem as clever either, which is unsurprising once you discover he was losing faith in the group. But then again, maybe I am judging this to earlier works just a little too closely. As a stand alone album, independent to the others, it's a lovely, gentle folk gem.

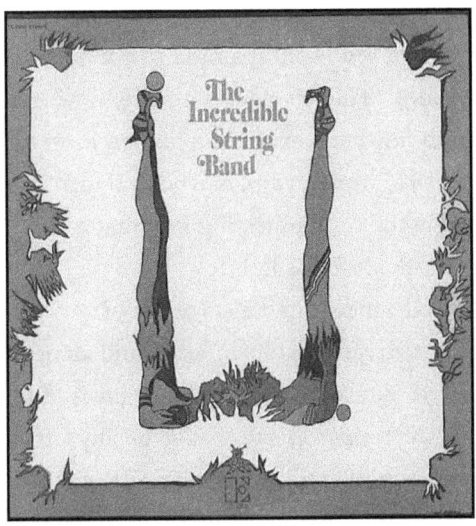

U

(1970)

In 1970, Williamson's grander visions reached a fruition when he and the ISB staged U, "a surreal parable of dance and song" at the London Roundhouse. The band had recently met the dance troupe Stone Monkey, who had originally come out of David Medalla's Exploding Galaxy group and the ideas for U were born out of this association. In truth Williamson was never just a songs man. He had been pushing to get a visual element into the band since The Pirate and the Crystal Ball movie. By 1968, role play and costumes had become an important part of their live shows. Heron, never too big a fan of this side of things, was still happy to go along with it all, perhaps reluctantly.

Janet Shankman designed all the sets, hand painted of course, and images were projected as slides. The concept, broadly, was the notion that a soul appears from nowhere, exists in a human form for a while, and then exits the physical world again, maybe to return in a new shell down the line. "Hence the U, manifesting into matter then re-ascending back into the great finale," says Robin.

And what of the whole physical concept of the stage show?

"Well, it was described as a surreal parable in song and dance," Williamson recalled. "The word 'dance' may have been misleading because the amount of dance in terms of, say, ballet or any other recognisable dance form was undoubtedly minimal. It was an example of a thing that we were interested in at the time, which you might call inspired amateurism. It was doing something very much off the cuff and it was an entertainment again designed originally primarily for friends and then taken out as an experiment to see how it would go. I've spoken to a number of people for whom it was their favourite album. We recorded the album in 48 hours and it is a double album. That's very quick. It was night and day for 48 hours. So you can see it was very much off the cuff. The story itself is of the loosest possible... It's called "U" because it's U in shape. It starts off with somebody in some ancient period of the Golden Age in the past, who survives successive lifetimes coming down through lesser and lesser awarenesses and finally gets back to a good state of mind again. That is about the whole plot. Now woven around that plot are as many little incidents, bizarre things and bits of humour as we could wind into it. Pretty light-hearted."

The critics were far from impressed, although Robin is adamant the fans loved it. Over in the US, they presented it in New York, but the tour was cancelled after a few performances, going down rather badly at Fillmore East. To recoup financial losses, Boyd got the band into the studio to record an album and yes, it was all done in 48 hours, with the band working in shifts, overdubbing pieces   and taking power naps while one of the other members laid down their parts. It must have been exhausting working under such conditions. However, this obvious pressure is not apparent when listening to the glorious music.

Boyd though was less than impressed by the new direction. He had, after all, loved the band as a duo, and seeing them going off into more ambitious areas worried him. "Their next two albums had some string tracks, but overall they were no match for the earlier ones," wrote Boyd. "They moved a group of dancers and Scientologist friends into the Row and created a pageant called U. I tried to discourage them. With a cast of ten plus sets and costumes, it was going to be very costly to tour. The lyrics were even more obscure than their opaque masterpieces of the past and the tunes weren't as good. The group refused to contemplate the notion of failure."

But when listening to the album, one can put all the complication to one side. Opening with a wonderful Heron piece, El Wool Suite, anyone expecting an impenetrable set of riddles and elaborate pieces is eased nicely into a purely soothing and fascinating musical environment. Heron's sitar playing is superb here, with the tempura buzzing away restlessly in the background. There's a lovely flute solo a few minute in, and one can only imagine what this music would have been like accompanied by the visual spectacles of the stage version. The song culminates in a bongo driven fusion of flute and Indian interplay, simply fantastic. It may be 8 minutes, but it's the kind of limitless, exciting, liberated piece of music you could have on throughout the whole day.

The Juggler's Song certainly brings us back into the eccentric and good humoured familiarity of classic ISB. The juggler himself, portrayed with theatrical brilliance by Robin on the recording, complete with rolling Rs, is a mischievous character delighting in his magic. "Something to blow your mind away" indeed. The song climaxes with a chilling psychedelic call of "Time..." And the Excellency continues on with, yes, Time, which sounds like it could have come straight off the 5000 Spirits album, some tasty exotic stringed patterns weaving and winding around Robin's voice with eloquence.

Another reason to love the U album is that it brings us a personal favourite of mine by the ISB, Queen of Love. Even outside of the U concept, like most of the tracks here, this can be taken solely as a Williamson gem. There's that brilliant chord sequence to start with, the gorgeous "chorus" part, and some irresistible flute and violin lines playing off each other. Plus there's the wonderfully imaginative lyrics, "should I now put lion's ears upon my own ears, hear every sound as a roar?"

At this point, I think it's fair to explore the literary merit of Robin's lyrics. Asked of his influences in this field by Pagan Dawn, Robin said "As a little boy, my granny used to read me Rudyard Kipling and I still love some of those stories, the Just So Stories and so on, and even though Kipling isn't frightfully fashionable nowadays at that time he was a wonderful influence, in the Just So Stories and the Mowgli stories particularly. But then of course the Brothers Grimm, I used to read them when I was a boy you know...." He went on to reiterate his love of Kerouac and the beat writers, plus influences from William Blake and other areas. "I loved the idea of spontaneous writing. People like Jack Kerouac and later on people like Charles Bukowski used to write in a very apparently spontaneous manner.

They would let the words flow, and I loved that, and it was only when I came across the poet William Blake that I got the idea that what he was talking about an inspired voice you see. The notion of the inspired voice which is a very Bardic sort of notion, and in a way that's a very traditional notion in the Celtic heritage of say Wales and Ireland."

Musically, the album continues in its eclectic joy, and considering we're talking about a band well known for their mixing of styles and ideas, U is certainly even more varied than expected. Unfortunately though it was not a hit and was deemed their biggest commercial disappointment yet. Even now, it's harder to find than their other works, which is a shame, for this is one of the cleverest, most joyful albums from an era where everything and everyone was starting to sound the same, with 15 minute guitar solos, spinning keyboards with daggers in them and elaborate drum solos. Shameless excess! Perhaps this is why such a gentle, and it has to be said often plain mad masterpiece like this can sink without trace. Shame.

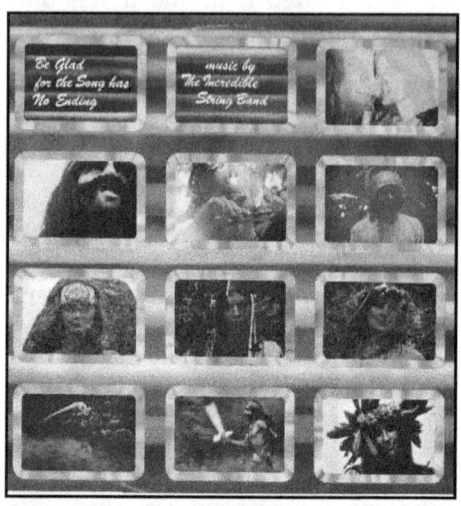

Be Glad For the Song Has No Ending (1971)

One of Boyd's last pieces of work for the band was this, the soundtrack to their classic movie Be Glad For the Song Has No Ending. Opening with Come With Me, the album doesn't get off to the perfect start, the shrill vocals of Licorice and screechy violin far from the ISB's finest moment. All Writ Down is much easier to get into, an inspired Robin guitar opening with cool bass line by Rose. A strong Heron/Williamson co-vocal leads the song blissfully.

The unforgettable mandolin music that opens the 26 minute epic The Song Has No Ending, by far the album's stand out, instantly brings to mind the pirate with the large painted on black moustache in the band's brilliant Crystal Ball movie, but the music itself, disconnected from the surreal visuals, still stands as a enjoyably eccentric experience. The Heron led chant that resurfaces now and then on the opener, leading us into a colourful world ahead is pure hippy holiness, the shaking of the tambourine, the thudding acoustic guitar, it all lifts the spirit and makes you think of that wonderful period in time where the String Band were giants.

The collection is a nice addition to the catalogue and although only the epic closer really blows you away, it stands as a document before a changing era for the band. A new phase was about to begin and musical dynamics were about to completely alter, for better or worse.

The exiting of Boyd changed things considerably too, but he simply couldn't see eye to eye with them anymore, and their refusal to listen to any of his advice was affecting relationships. He hated Scientology, the "jargon" attached to it and the cost he felt it was having on the group. He appointed Suzie Watson-Taylor to see to their affairs and left them to it. Still, he found their new life style bizarre and was losing faith in their material.

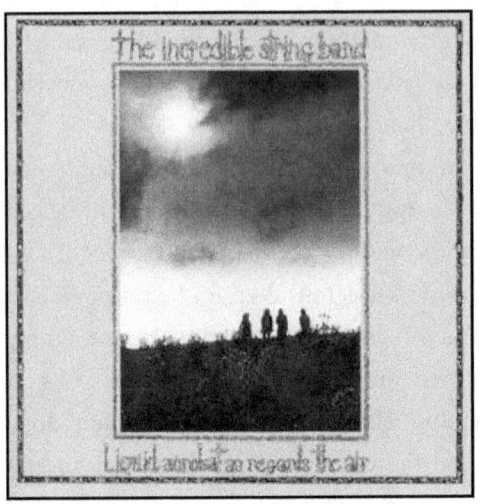

Liquid Acrobat as Regards the Air (1971)

All good things come to an end, or at least they eventually do, and on the way they definitely change. By 1971, the classic four piece line up was to dissolve, when Rose lost interest in the band and left. Here, Malcolm LeMaistre of Stone Monkey entered the picture as a proper member of the group. Having previously worked with the band on The Pirate and the Crystal Ball, he was trusted to bring his own unique and very different style into the music, even though he had very little prior experience as a musician prior to this. The ISB were moving on it seemed.

Dynamics have clearly changed from the first bars of Talking of the End, where the ISB actually has what can be best described as a stomping rhythm section, something they rarely had before with their free form melodies floating up and down, but soon it develops into classic ISB territory with its creepy, almost ceremonial chant, then lots of bells, toms and percussion come in to bring it to life. It's a wonderfully varied song, and although sonically quite different for the band, it's like a welcome breath of fresh air. Then of course we have the characteristic high Licorice vocals and Heron sitar lines.

Dear Old Battlefield is more like 70s Donovan than the ISB, but it's a cool and quite groovy Williamson track, with some nice electric guitar work. Heron and Licorice's Cosmic Boy is a daft vaudeville style number, with Rose calling out to her cosmic boy against a great piano shuffle. Heron's first sole penned track on the album is Worlds They Rise and Fall, a powerful power ballad with a very strong vocal from the man himself.

Heron shines elsewhere, especially with the electric Painted Chariot, a genuine stand out from the ISB 70s catalogue. Surprisingly, he proves to be a great rock singer, and the chorus is brilliant, a lost classic chant that's so catchy everyone should hear it. The cymbal heavy drums, electric strums and booming bass blast out from the speakers completely unexpectedly, before the listener is taken into more mysterious territory, the "find the wise players" chant, then with the heavy 60s Jefferson Airplane style organ stabs. It leads into a totally enthralling rock out section, a genuine psychedelic freak out. Brilliant.

Red Hair is one of Heron's sweeter and more typical numbers, a pretty tune with a touching melody and violin part; simplistic, bare and quick, it's over in little over 2 minutes (although you can always press repeat).

The album's closer is the epic Darling Belle, a Williamson oddity with a great Licorice vocal. Opening with "off to see the swans", we are instantly lost in a magical, wonderful story, with a lush arrangement. Williamson, Le Maistre and Licorice all share out the vocals on what is clearly a song about two characters communicating with each other.

"I wrote 'Darling Belle' very quickly," Robin said of the closing opus. "Or rather, wrote it down very quickly. I was lying in a hotel room in Rotterdam just before I fell asleep, and I began to hear these voices outside my head, and they were telling the story of Belle and James. Two voices, a man and a woman, and of what they said I jotted down fragments and the following morning I wrote parts of the song; about four months later I wrote the rest. It only lasted a few moments."

Production wise, it's clear that Boyd is no longer on board. It's hard to describe the difference in mixing, but there is an apparent shift. With Boyd, it felt closer, as if the band were crammed into a tiny cupboard and playing right before you, voices clear, not much frills, basic and wonderfully under-produced. There's a difference here with Stanley Schier's take on the band, and the result is typical of the 1970s sound. Considering people often remark that this is the point the material took a turn for the worst, I myself can't see their point. It's a fresh sounding record, full of new ideas, a blending of rock, folk and plain uncategorisable ISB uniqueness.

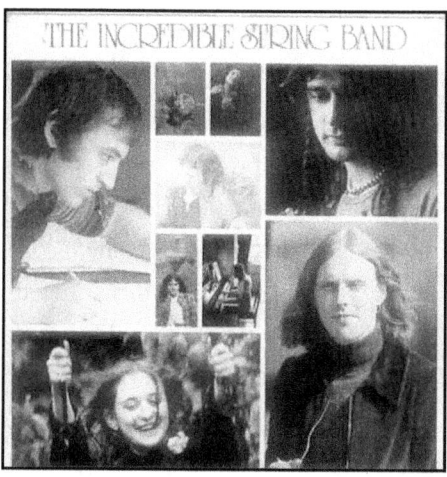

Earthspan

(1972)

In 1972, even more fresh blood was to enter the ISB camp. Earthspan was produced by Roger Mayer and band wise, Gerard Dott was also now on board, along with Stan Schnier (who had produced Liquid Acrobat...) who took on the bass and Jack Ingram on drums.

Opening with Le Maistre's My Father Was a Lighthouse Keeper, the album doesn't get off to a very good start. Le Maistre's vocal tends to grate a little and the whole melody doesn't really connect with me as a listener. However, Le Maistre's Sailor and the Dancer is a nice little song, with some lovely accordion and classic Likky vocals. Still, there is the slightest hint they are trying to recapture something that is eluding them, the old ISB magic perhaps.

Likky and Heron co wrote Sunday Song. While Likky's voice is brilliant when backing, it can grate a little when over used, as it often does on this album. But once this one gets going it's quite a decent song, if a tad depressing. Williamson and Le Maistre's The Actor is OK but forgettable and in fact only Banks of Sweet Italy has a hint of classic ISB, although in the 1970s it could have sounded more like a nostalgic revisit than a reimagining. However, as soon as Williamson's familiar tones come in, like an old friend you had almost forgotten about, the song really strikes a chord. Williamson's Restless Night is a nice, almost jazzy number, with a quirky melody and vocal delivery by Robin. There's a nice sound to the acoustic guitars and the keyboards, and the occasional calls of Likky add a nice touch.

Once again, as is often the case, they end the album on a high note, here with Heron's powerful Seagull. If there is one problem with the album as a whole though, in my opinion of course, then it is this. The ISB were at their best when Robin and Mike interplayed and competed with each other, creating a magical chemistry that was truly unique. Apart, there is a strange void in the music, rather like splitting Lennon and McCartney, dimming out the bright lights that sparked between them. Hearing them both together, vocally and musically, conjures a wonderful feeling it is hard to define. Here, they may be on the record together, but they rarely sound "together", and that is maybe what makes this album pass you by rather than grab your heart.

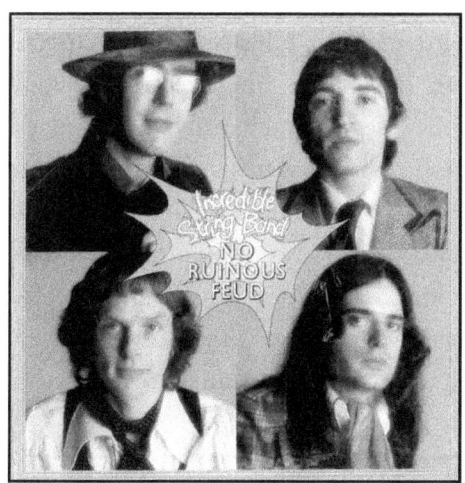

No Ruinous Feud
(1973)

Likky had now left the band, and in her wake, the ISB lost much of their quirky charm. Going on as a more solid straight forward rock outfit, No Ruinous Feud is brighter than the rather weak Earthspan, but is still a far cry from their finest work. Explorer is a strong opener though, sounding similar to Cat Stevens' material at that point, complete with female backing singers and a thumping drum back beat. It has Heron in his transitional period from folk rocker to songwriter of the 70s and 80s, and is a strong number, his vocals in particular being very strong indeed. Le Maistre's Down Before Cathay is a nice pleasant ballad, while Williamson's Saturday Maybe is perhaps the album's strongest point. Old Buccaneer however doesn't quite work for me, with its cheesy screeching saxophones jarring awkwardly with Robin's fine voice. At the Lighthouse Dance, another Le Maistre song is a more funky number with weird synths, female backing vocals and a groovy rhythm. It's certainly interesting to say the least and sounds very much of its time. Heron's Turquoise Blue is a nice percussive number, despite often sounding like music that accompanied the Carry On films (images of Sid James nipping Barbara Windsor's arse flashed in my mind for some reason, or maybe I am just pervy). Heron's melody is pleasant and it brings much relief after the misguided experimentation that has come before it. Perhaps the most curious cut here is their cover of Dolly Parton's My Blue Tears, but Williamson's Weather the Storm is perhaps the worst song he wrote for the ISB.

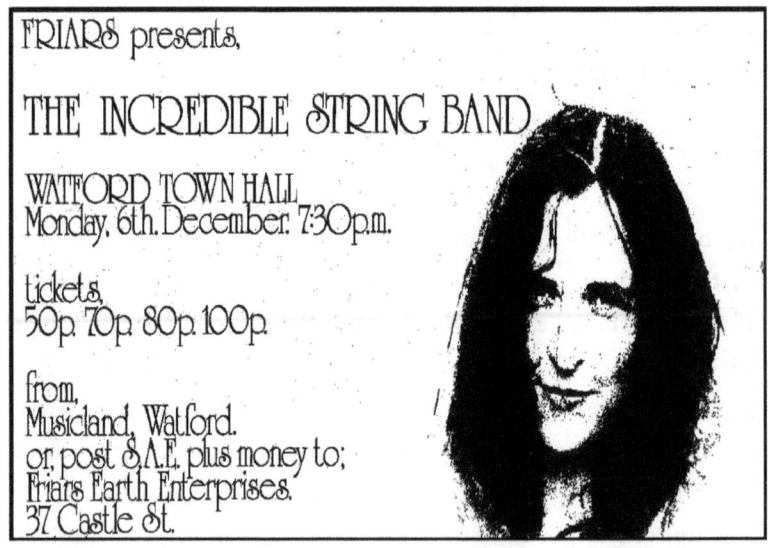

FRIARS presents,

THE INCREDIBLE STRING BAND

WATFORD TOWN HALL
Monday, 6th. December. 7:30p.m.

tickets,
50p 70p 80p 100p

from,
Musicland, Watford.
or, post S.A.E. plus money to;
Friars Earth Enterprises.
37 Castle St.

Finishing off with Little Girl, a genuinely nice Heron song, you get the feeling that listening to No Ruinous Feud is more of a task than a pleasure, the odd mix of eclectic styles not quite gelling as they should. Thankfully, in my view, their next record was their strongest since Liquid Acrobat...

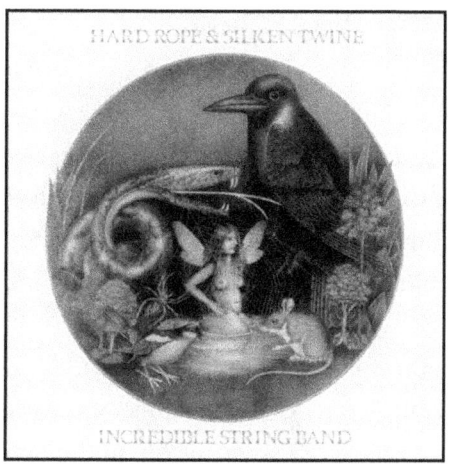

Hard Rope and
Silken Twine
(1974)

By 1973, the ISB were barely recognisable as the outlaw, flower hippies of 1968. But in 1974, they were to recapture some of their former glory, with Stan Schnier on bass, Jack Ingram on the drums and adding Graham Forbes on electric guitar. A band has to develop and move on in order to stay fresh, and had the ISB stuck to the exact formula of their early records, people, fans or not, would still have criticised their decision to stand still creatively.

Forbes, an accomplished guitarist who has gone on to write books about his musical adventures, told me how he got involved with the ISB.

"I bumped into Mike Heron by chance in London," he said to me. "I had a rock band in Glasgow at the time (Powerhouse). I knew Mike had made a rocky solo album and offered my band as session musicians for his next one, telling him we'd be a lot cheaper than the Who and Jimmy Page (who he'd used on Smiling Men With Bad Reputations). He invited me to Glen Row to record some songs. I had no idea I was being tried out for the ISB. He then asked if I'd be up for a 3 month tour which was starting in 10 days time. I had to think for about 1 second!"

How did Graham get on with them musically and personally?

"I really liked Mike and Robin," says Graham. "Mike was very focused, very organised, had a very clear vision of his music and where he wanted to go. In my opinion he should have been the UK's Springsteen. He was writing great rock material which we did with the String Band... I liked Robin
very much too. He was very much into esoteric things, and was an expert on Celtic folklore. A totally fascinating guy to talk to. They were both great musicians, especially Robin. He could literally play anything. Let's not forget Malcolm. He was like an absent minded professor; very clever, very knowledgeable, wrote interesting songs and was also a real character."

Although the album had its rockier moments, perhaps due to Graham and Mike's influence, there were moments in the band's repertoire that sounded like ye olde ISB, as Graham agreed.

"I am very pleased with Dreams of No Return where I am playing acoustic guitar and the song is very much the 'old ISB'. There is a live BBC recording of that on an album somewhere, although the date on it I think is wrong. I always preferred playing live rather than recording. I've never really liked recording. I have some recordings which may or may not be on compilations, I don't know because I never listen to anything I am playing on. I wrote a small part of Ithkos (the album's closer); actually it was an old Powerhouse thing. The music I played with the band was of course very different to the 60s stuff."

Were the band losing fans due to the shift in sound?

"Most definitely we weren't losing fans," says Graham. "Quite the opposite. Some older fans reacted much like Dylan's fans did when he went electric, but really the band had always been very experimental and eager to try new music, so doing the electric stuff was very much in keeping with the spirit of the early band. We did a big UK tour with McGuiness Flint supporting us. They had a No1 hit with When I'm Dead and Gone so the gigs had a lot of younger people who really had come to see them, but stayed because we were headlining. They absolutely loved the rocky stuff, and went crazy when we did jigs and reels, especially since we were doing them with a much more driving feel. Our fan base was getting bigger and bigger. We did Drury Lane in Feb 1974 and 2 coach loads of new young fans came down from Newcastle, as well as hundreds from the London area. We totally sold out that gig, in fact I was told there were about 2000 over the gig capacity – it was before health and safety and the doormen just let people in. There wasn't an inch of space in the hall, stairways, everything crammed. In true ISB fashion though, the tour manager didn't give the music press guest passes and what was really a massive gig was never written about in the press. When we toured America, the crowds absolutely loved the new electric stuff. We seemed all set to take off there in a very big way. So while the old stuff was great, and I persuaded Robin to do things like First Girl on the last US tour and to close the show with This Moment with just Mike and Robin alone, there is no doubt in my mind that the fan base was getting far bigger. We were moving from being a cult band to one with a very big mainstream following when the band split up." Joe Boyd and others have claimed that Williamson and Heron could no longer see eye to eye. Graham, a man who was there, has a different take on matters.

"I never saw them arguing," he told me. "Not once, and I spent a lot of time on the road with them and living with them at the Row. They seemed to have a great respect for each others' music even though it was quite different. Mike was much more rock-orientated, Robin acoustic. I loved touring with the band, loved it, especially when John Gilston joined on drums. We were all quite different...I was very young... but we all got on very well. I honestly cannot recall a single argument. They were nice people, all of them. Susie Watson-Taylor was the best manager I have ever known. She was tremendous with people."

Listening to the album myself, ignoring any comparisons to older styles, I find Hard Rope and Silken Twine a really enjoyable experience. Granted it is almost totally unrecognizable as the band that did 5000 Spirits, but there is some stellar songwriting here. The opener, Heron's Maker of Islands is a beautiful song, a perfect Mike melody with a lovely string arrangement in the back and towards the finale. It's easy to see how his songs were covered by numerous artists in the 70s and 80s. His vocal on it too is spot on, illustrating what a fantastic voice he really has. Williamson's Cold February, recorded live in concert, is a brilliant track, sounding at once that it could be both vintage ISB and a song written hundreds of years ago. Its gorgeous flute line and haunting sad melody is reminiscent of the Dubliners' version of the Unquiet Grave. From these two opening tracks, we can clearly see how far Heron and Williamson's tastes had come and it's pretty hard to think of two more different songs in style than these.

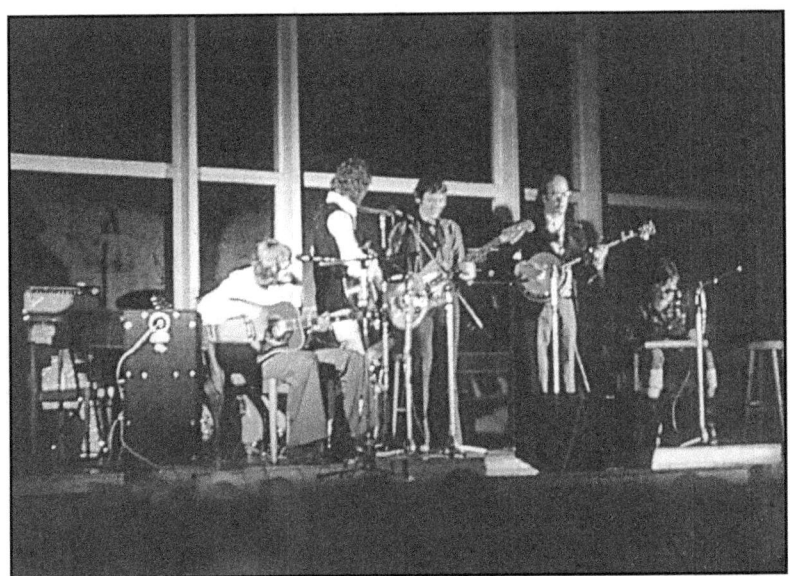

Le Maistre's Glancing Love is yet another shade of colour this album has, with its soulful vocal, nice organ and guitar interplay. Hardly the strongest moment on the album however, it's still a pleasant track. Williamson's Dreams of No Return hints towards the older ISB material, yet it has a slightly more conventional 70s arrangement, with its haunting vocal, cello and for good measure, lovely sitar part by Mike. Heron's Dumb Kate, another live recording, is like a wound up Log Cabin Home in the Sky. A ragged violin jig, with shouting vocals from Heron and Le Maistre, it's the one sole weak point for me.

Album closer Ithkos is brilliant from the start; beginning with a jaunty yet thorough Walt Disney-esque bouncing string arrangement, it boasts some superb guitar work from Forbes. A slight Indian feel is apparent in the second minute, while the whole thing moves along into its gentler string section. Then we have the bongo driven groove, the fluid guitar lines playing against the wailing wild flute, like songbirds going crazy in the sky. Then there's the very seventies but brilliantly recorded electric guitar bursting in at 3 minutes, with stadium rock organ stabs and thudding tom toms. The piece progresses from here, with rock solos side by side with some inventive violin, before the vocals come in. It's a lost epic prog rock classic, and not something most people would expect from the ISB, that's for sure.

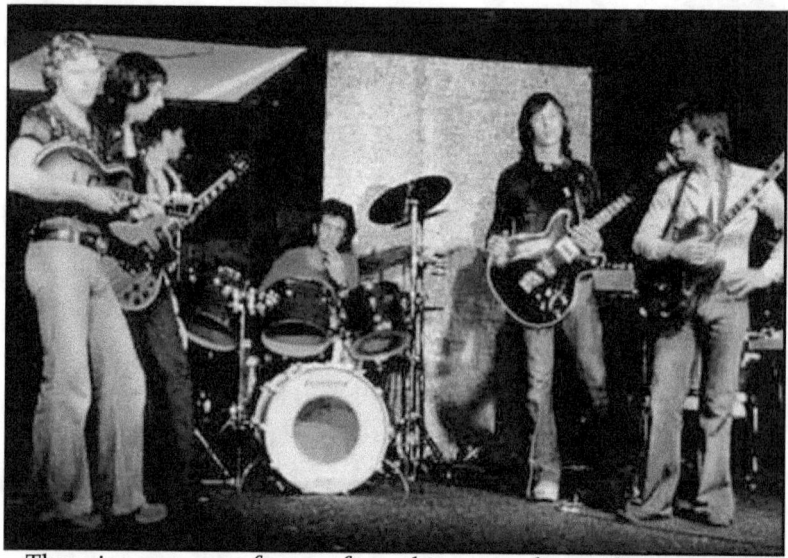

There is some great footage from this era, and considering we don't have much ISB footage available, save a few TV appearances and the Be Glad film, it's pretty cool stuff. The "rehearsal" film as it is known was made by James Archibald and one interesting segment shows them rehearsing the epic Ithkos. There's Mike explaining the genesis of the track. "The group looked like it needed a larger vehicle to try out its combined skills on," Heron explains in voice over. "If I could get a large enough piece, scope and canvas for people to really get into it and paint what they wanted on the large canvas of it. So that was the thought in my mind. The theme is the corruption of myth characters put together with fiction.... this travelling merchant called Ithkos, an adventuring kind of guy." Robin seems dissatisfied with the piece, calling the segments "vastly too long". Once can see Williamson is far from happy with the direction of the material, adding that his interest wasn't held by the piece, and his facial expression alone is worth a thousand words. After all, Ithkos is as far away from Robin's tastes as one can get.

The recording environment however seems idyllic, the row of Scottish cottages and the freedom of the recording sessions looks like a heavenly set up for a musician. Although it may often be uncomfortable viewing, the Rehearsal footage is compelling and treasured among fans, a rare glimpse into the ISB's creative process.

When you see a clip like this, one simply has to acknowledge those seemingly outlandish statements by Joe Boyd. "Mike and Robin were Clive's friends rather than each other's," he once wrote. "Without him as a buffer, they developed a robust dislike for one another. Fortunately the quantity and quality of their song writing was roughly equal." By this time though, the song writing did not seem equal, nor did either seem comfortable with the other "imposing" himself on their song.

Although not without fans, especially when listening to Graham's views, their recordings from this era are now considered disappointments in comparison to the older material. It's easier too for the press to keep an act pigeonholed into a neat little package. But the ISB, as Graham stated, were always about progressing and would not be slaves to labels and tags.

In late 1974, they were dropped from Island. There are claims of course that Heron and Williamson weren't getting on musically and in October of that year, they decided to call it a day and went on to pursue their own solo careers. You only have to take a look at live footage of the time, seeing an uncomfortable Williamson on electric violin, that this folk rock fusion wasn't going to last.

"Well the final tour for us ended in America, New York in fact," Heron later recalled. "Robin just decided to leave at that point. At that point it was stretching his ... I mean if you've seen what he's doing now you can probably understand how painful it was to be involved in that era that was going so hard towards ... because the thing is you've got a band with a conventional rock format and you've got one guy who's folkie and one who's into rock, no matter how you try to share the leadership the band is going to go towards the rock guy because he's running much more for them. So that is what was happening and he was like having to get his wee bit in because the band was gradually becoming more of a rock band, so he was put in a position where he couldn't continue without compromising himself really and we agreed that neither of us would use the name, I mean the String Band wasn't me or him, it was a chemistry and to continue without either of us would have been really dishonest, so we just agreed to dump it."

"I was very disappointed," Graham said of the split. "At the end of the last US tour, we were about to sign with a new label in America who realised we were on the brink of huge commercial success. Robin and Mike stayed in New York to discuss the deal with the label owner. Mike and Robin disagreed on the future direction of the band, and Mike called me to say the band had broken up and would I help him put a new band together? That was how Mike Heron's Reputation came about. Some of the Reputation songs were songs we had played on the last ISB tour....Strong Thing, Draw Back the Veil etc."

In 1979, Williamson spoke of his own view on the disintegration of the band. "Well, I think that Mike was always more interested in the electric music than I was. I never had much interest in it. Originally when we first met him, he'd been playing in what you might call blue beat bands or early Mod bands and he always maintained an interest in that, which I think gradually surfaced as the band developed, but one of the things that I most enjoyed about the change is that - I mean, the reason that I wanted to leave the band - I wanted to get back into acoustic music and more folk-based music and I'm probably playing stuff that's folkier now than anything I've done in a long, long time; it's all pretty much an attempt to write new traditional music really and I'm writing new songs, but in what I conceive to be a fairly traditional way. Very traditional structures, all kinds of traditional instrumentation too. "

Although it may be controversial to blame Scientology for the band's creative shift, it is also been addressed so frequently that you can barely ignore it. Clearly, things did change when Scientology entered their world, but it was something that Mike had decided to stay clear of by the late 1980s, years after the ISB had split up. When asked in the 80s why though, Mike wasn't being overly telling.

"Well I'm completely out," he said. "Four years I've been completely out. The only reason I do want to say anything about it is that if I was used as a reason to get people in - then I would say something about it, but otherwise I feel it's just totally a personal thing, and the fact that I'm in or out shouldn't influence anyone. But I've just disconnected a couple of years ago and I've nothing to do with it anymore. It's just a personal philosophy some people find useful."

Scientologists or not, it seemed to be the end of the ISB story.

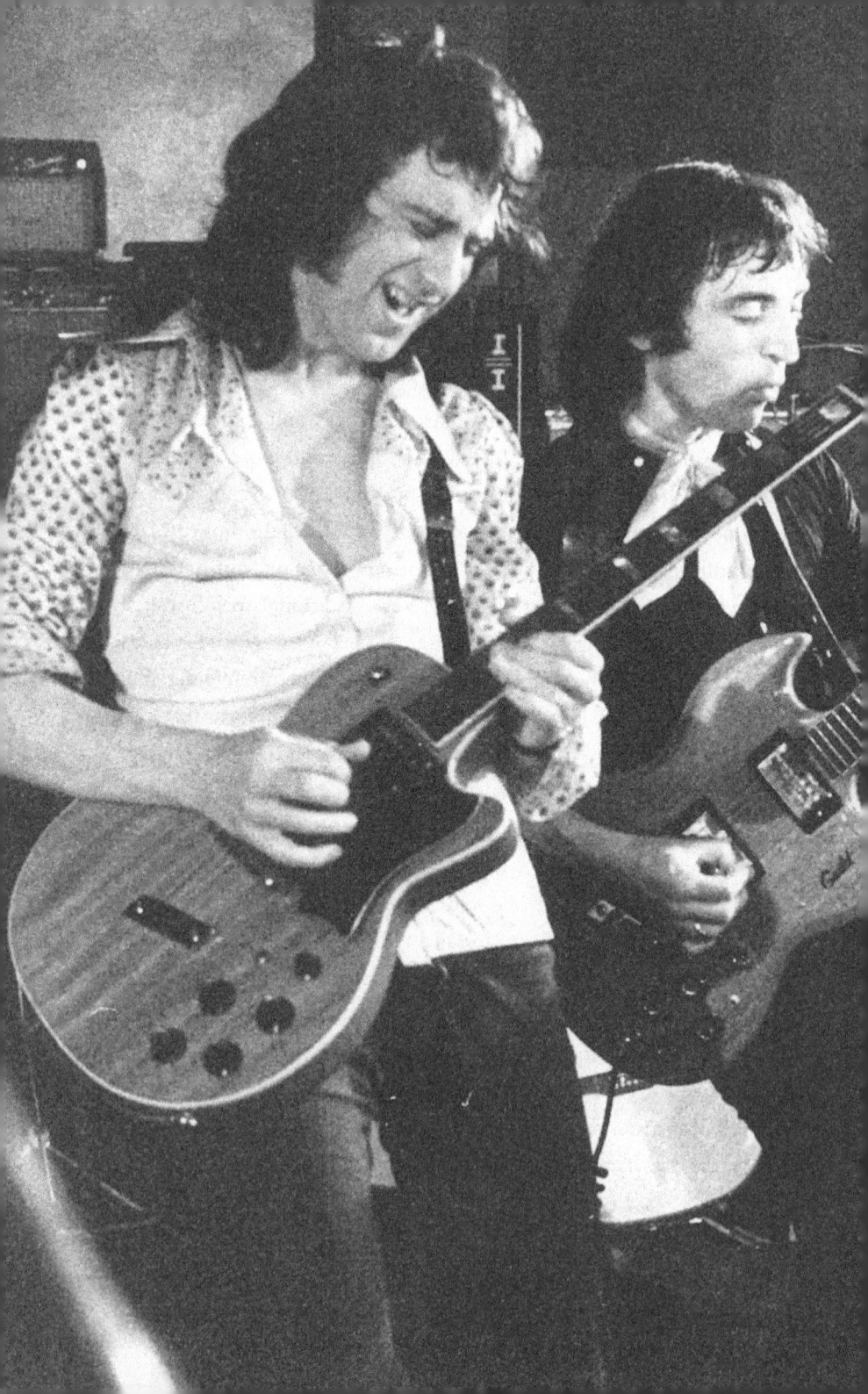

ITY HALL, GLASGOW
HURSDAY, 28 OCTOBER at 7.30

TICKETS : £1.10, 90p, 80p, 70p, 60p

om Cuthbertons Box Office. 21 Cambridge St. Glasgow C2
Tel: 332 5382

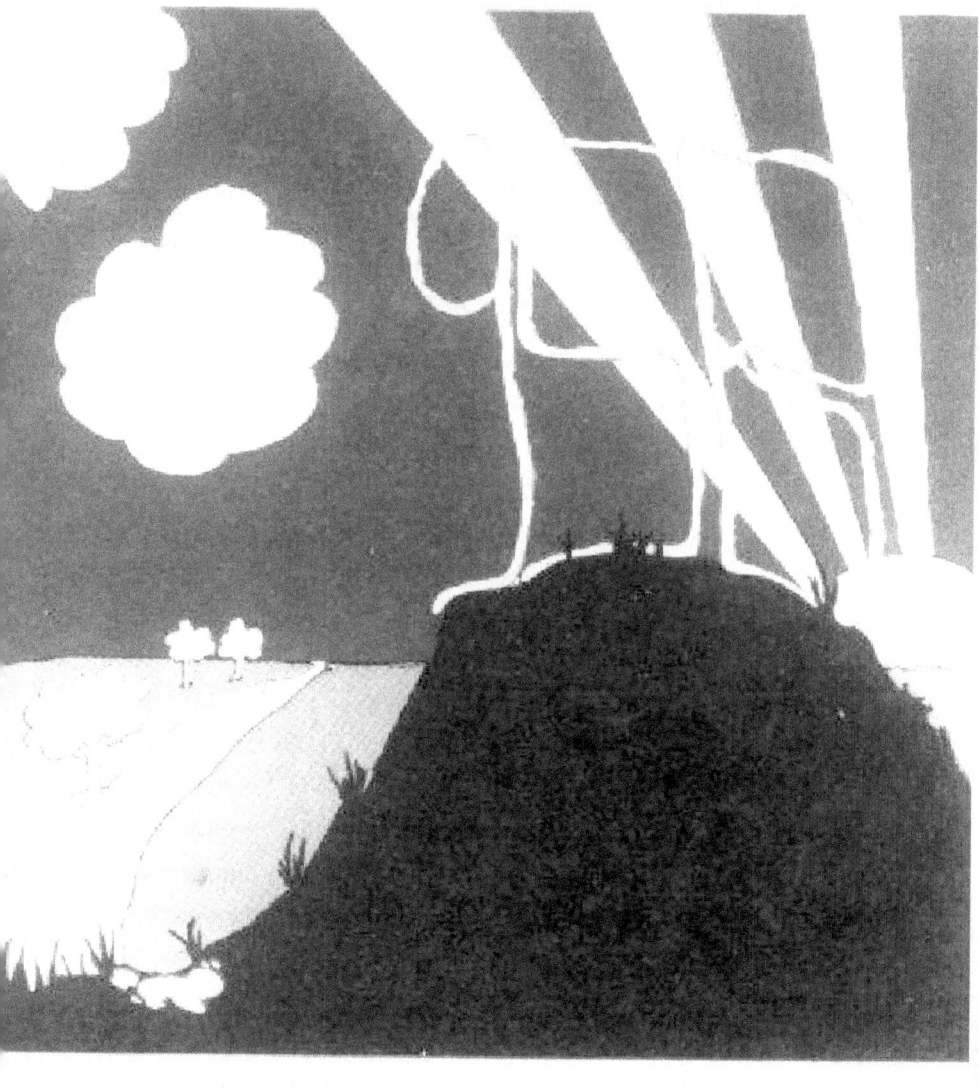

INCREDIBLE STRING BAND

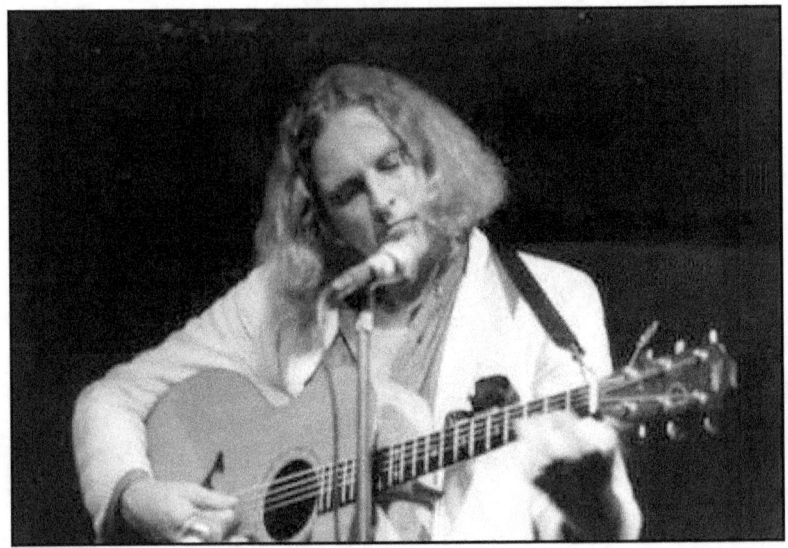

After the ISB

In the dark streets of Hyde Park, Leeds, in March 2013, a mixed gathering of excited and curious folk queue for what feels like two hours (it was only 10 minutes really) in the freezing cold to see the legendary Mike Heron, who is special guest tonight with acclaimed folk outfit The Trembling Bells. In a telling moment, Heron, a musical idol to many here tonight calmly passes the endless line of blue faces, smiles casually and strolls inside. This one tiny moment is rather telling and sums Mike up perfectly I feel. No ego, no stopping or waiting for awed gasps from his many followers, just a smile. In turn, the fans do not hound him, do not crowd him or ask him to sign LPs they have pulled from the dark depths of their raincoats. There will be none of that tonight.

Then we are inside, the polite punters handing over little receipt tickets and heading through the doors. I like this place, a classic old time cinema; one screen, small little hallway and counter that serves bottled beer, popcorn and sweets. It reminded me of my childhood when my Grandmother ran one of the last old fashioned cinemas in Leeds. Then we were seated, dad and I, right in the middle on the end of one of the rows. Perfect, except for the fact that we had to move every five minutes when someone needed the toilet or was off for another beverage. Oh well, we didn't mind, it only added a little farcical mayhem to it all. On top of this, the toilet down in the cellar was so small, men stood shoulder to shoulder at the urinals as nervous chaps with eyes facing to the ground awaited their turns, their bodies pressed right up against the backs of the men who were peeing. An awkward silence muffling on the tiled walls. Getting in and out and towards the tiny sink was comedic. One tall man with a beard smiled to me and laughed "it's like the Marx Brothers". He had a point, that fella.

The support act Stephanie Hladowski & C Joynes, play a haunting and enjoyable set, and then the lights go down. After a brief break, we are treated to a projection of the classic documentary on the Incredible String Band, a film which captures the naivety and creativity of that special time in music. It also reminds us of the sheer brilliance of the man who will soon be coming on stage. We were easing more and more into our seats as the night went by.

Then The Trembling Bells set up. They are a cool looking gang, good humoured and instantly warming, led by Lavinia Blackwall on vocals in a long gown, chatty drummer Alex Nielsen and multi instrumentalist Mike Hastings. As soon as they play a note they win you over, a collective sound that soothes and melds together to create unusual waves of invention. And Mike Heron, the man who played Woodstock and influenced thousands of musicians, simply smiles and leans on a beam at the back of the stage modestly, closing his eyes in bliss, and exchanging joyful glances with the band. But the real magic starts when he joins them at the front of the stage, and the moment we hear that familiar voice of his sends shivers down the spine. A Very Cellular Song was arguably the pinnacle of the night, with the whole band working together and spreading joy throughout the old cinema, but in such a perfect, relaxed and peaceful evening, picking out a highlight is impossible. Experiencing this gig makes me feel like the ISB story has come full circle.

In his years since the band split in 1974, Heron has pursued many avenues, and even occasionally gets back together with his ISB comrades, whether it be Williamson or Palmer, or both for that matter. The first Williamson and Heron reunion was in the mid 1990s, but it was received in a mixed fashion. Some were

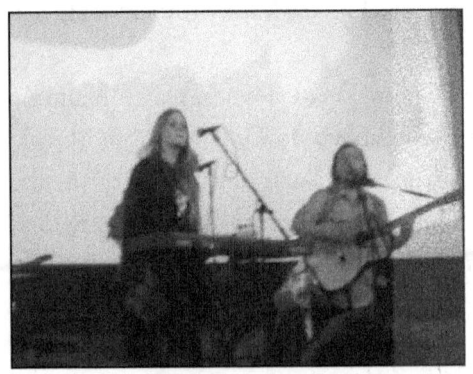

disappointed that the material seemed more conventional and that they chose few tracks from the "classic" era. Once again, they weren't keen on resting on their laurels.

These days though, you may catch Mike with his new compadres, the Trembling Bells, who he is often touring with up and down the country. It may help of course that his daughter plays keyboards for them and also that they are a very capable bunch of lads and lasses, replicating the spirit of the ISB quite closely. Mike told Bang Showbiz: "Well I am kind of stuck with getting old. But one of the nice things I get is I get to do a lot of work with my daughter. She keeps me young."

This aside, seeing Heron in concert in the 2000s is a highly positive and unforgettable experience; the way the man smiles and feels the love in the room, delights in the sounds and the general vibe, is something you really need to experience before you can understand it. Putting the joy he exudes into words only sounds corny, I admit that. but being there is something else.

In 1987, Heron was asked about his legacy with what the magazine Beat the Retreat called a "mythological band" like ISB. Heron was suitably modest of course.

"Well I think it was a unique band and I think it springs from that, and I think the combination- sometimes you get an odd combination. Me and Robin I think sparked off something that was right for that era. It's like you happen to hit something that marks an era, but other than that I don't feel 'mythical''. I'm very proud, I loved the whole development. My own particular favourites, I love the first one because it's like the band is totally uninfluenced, it's like what they should be doing rather than what's psychedelically the "in" thing or what people should be thinking: it's just a completely pure and innocent kind of record of us, and I like that one particularly. All the other albums, I like a couple of songs at least, but for one album, I could sit down, it wouldn't be torture for me to listen to the album several times, whereas I would probably wince a bit at some of the stuff on the late albums."

Robin of course exists in his own box to this day. Immediately after the ISB he started Robin Williamson and His Merry Band, before disbanding them and going out on his own, returning to his strong folk routes and gigging extensively in America, his home base for some time. Touring regularly to this day, either alone or with his wife Bina, Williamson's post ISB career has been widely varied and equally acclaimed. Taking a look at his 40 plus solo album credits shows that Williamson is far from done just yet.

"I like some of the ISB stuff although I regard much of it as juvenilia," he later remarked. "I am certainly not stuck in the 60s but the psychedelic thing meant so much more than drugs. To me it was tapping into the world in a very specific way. A lot of good came out of that period. The trappings may have fallen by the wayside but the ideas are still good."

So what of the girls? Well, that's another story. Rose had brief flings with Joe Boyd and even David Crosby, and had an ambition of becoming a sound engineer. Instead she started a family and seemingly went on to live a quiet life. Funnily enough she became the Mayoress of Aberystwyth in the 1990s and now lives near the Welsh town in a cottage.

Licorice, or Likky as she is often known, seems to have drifted off somewhere and nobody seems to know where. After leaving the ISB she made an appearance at a Scientology event in 1974 and joined Robin's Merry Band in the later part of the 70s for a brief spell. Divorcing from musician Brian Lambert, the 1980s seemed a strange decade for Likky. Brian's brother Michael sent a letter to an ISB fan site, claiming "They (Likky and Brian) got amicably divorced back in the late 70s or early 80s, maintained contact for a while after that and then drifted apart. Brian hasn't heard from her in years and has no idea where she may be. I recall my ex sister-in-law with fondness."

In truth, Likky hasn't been heard of since 1990, which is now 23 years, with one source claiming she took a walk in the California desert and never returned. According to other internet sources, Likky's sister has tried relentlessly to track her down, even hiring private detectives to attempt to do so. A nameless man, who seems to be obsessed in finding her, seemed certain in 2008 that he knew she was alive and well, but didn't disclose why or how he knew this. Williamson recently admitted that she may have died, but as there is no evidence. In truth, Likky's disappearance remains one of pop's great mysteries. Will she ever surface? Well, Syd Barrett's legendary Madcap Laughs cover buddy Iggy the Eskimo did return in 2012 after what seemed to be a 40 year absence from existence, so you never know. One can only hope.

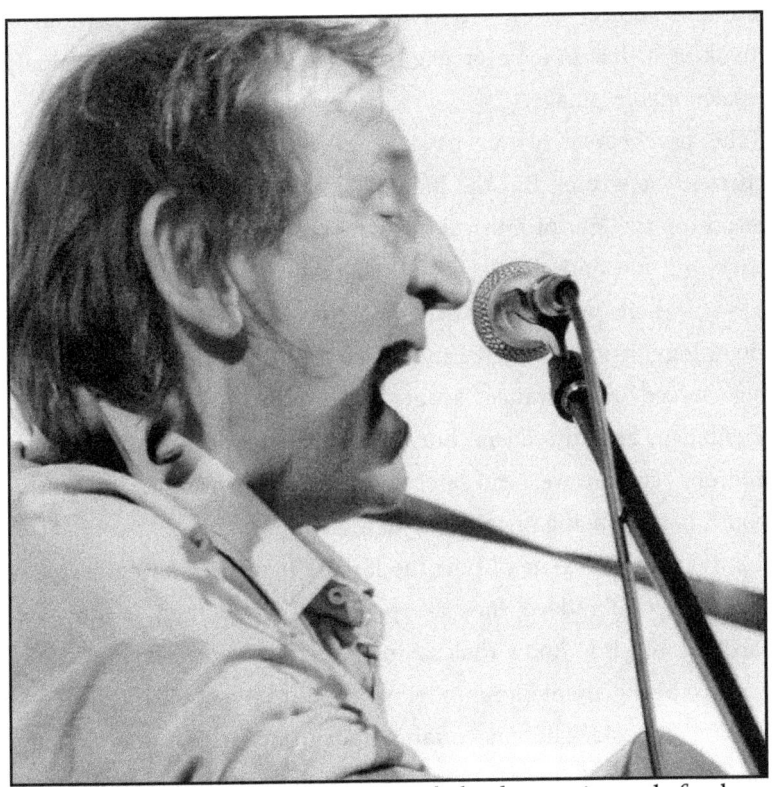

Although the band has a strong and slowly growing cult fandom, I still believe they are vastly under rated. Like Donovan, they have unfairly become stereotypes of their decade, despite the expansion of back catalogues, easily available CDs and retrospectives bringing their brilliant work into the new millennium. For some reason, maybe due to the narrow minded press, we are not taking their music as simply music, but are almost being forced to accept it as a product firmly of its time. This is the flaw in modern listening, in the throw away culture we have today. It's so easy to dismiss, to turn off after a few seconds and play some programmed, pro-tooled nonsense and turn it up loud!

On the subject of the ISB's legacy, Joe Boyd wrote a thought provoking article in 1997 for The Guardian discussing their decidedly "unfashionable" image.

"The psychedelic Sixties have again become fashionable in the Nineties," he wrote. "But the Incredible String Band has remained in the un-hip twilight of musical history - partly because of their folksy image, but not entirely. Perhaps the lack of recognition has more to do with their precipitous decline following their 'conversion' to Scientology in 1968. When I met Mike and Robin in 1965, they had long served as advance scouts into the territories of drugs, Orientalism and mysticism, but they were far from mindless flower children. They were, still are, highly intelligent and thoughtful people, besides being inventive and original musicians."

I am not sure in general how the ISB are perceived to the everyday pop listener, if indeed they are perceived at all (and if this even matters), but I do know that having seen a Mike Heron show, there seems to be a general like-mindedness about the people interested in the band's music. There is certainly no agro, no posers there for the "hip factor", no hangers on or bandwagon jumpers. People seem relaxed, there for the good time, the music and the joy of uplifting songs. Still, surprisingly a lot of young people were among the crowd, who have no doubt discovered their delights on You Tube, Spotify and the blogging world of the internet. Perhaps then, the attitudes towards the Incredible String Band have at least started to change, even if Boyd's hasn't. A more recent Guardian article by him included such statements as this:

"For a couple of years, managing the ISB, I made all the right calls. But I lost my touch somewhere around 1969, letting the ISB come back to Woodstock on the Saturday afternoon and fall flat in the baking sunshine, thereby missing out on the film and the live album. The group went into decline, I left for California to work for Warner Brothers, and, despite all the revivals of 60s music, the Incredible String Band were to remain stuck in people's minds as hopelessly hippie and embarrassingly flowery, like Maharishi-era Beatles. That Paul McCartney called their third album, The Hangman's Beautiful Daughter, album of the year in 1968, and the Stones tried to sign them to their label, have long been forgotten. Of all the groups of the 60s, they have the highest ratio of past success to current anonymity."

They may exist in the shadow of such 1960s icons as The Beatles, Led Zeppelin or The Rolling Stones, but they unarguably left a big impression on all three and perhaps best symbolise the most honest aspect of that decade of free love, the discovery of drugs, naïve exploration and musical liberation. Robin is as far from a commercially minded musician as you can get, and I am sure his goal was never to get a Number One record! They didn't and still don't make their music for fashion; they made it because they wanted to. And that, of course, is why they remain unique.

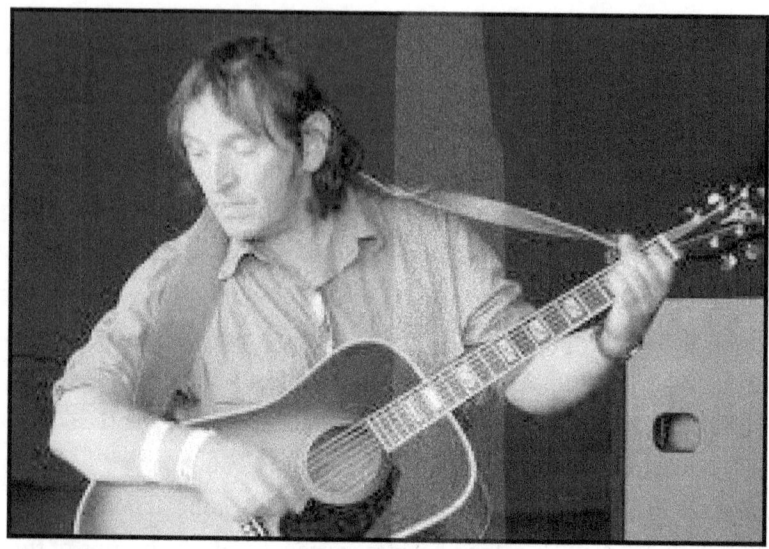

A Word with Mike Heron

Chris Wade fires a few questions Mike's way. The Man himself on his favourite of the band's records, The Hangman's Beautiful Daughter and ISB in general...

You have said in the past that the first album was one of the best ISB records, for its purity and rawness. Do you still like the album?

The first album is not really my favourite but it represents what happened when Robin, Clive and myself put together a band and a repertoire. It brings back memories of meetings, places, taking the show we'd made around the folk clubs, and finally the three of us in a circle at Sound Techniques studios round a clutch of microphones making an album in a day. So I have warm feelings for it.

The 5000 Spirits album was quite radically different. How do you look back on the making of that album?

Robin went off to Morocco and Clive to India; the band had really broken up. Six months later Robin returned inspired and carrying lots of North African instruments and a bundle of songs. The two of us played the songs we'd written on our holidays and thus was born 5000 Spirits. We still recorded in Sound Techniques, but using a different recording method. We would put down a basic song and embroider it with overdubs.

How do you look back on the Hangman's Beautiful Daughter album?

Hangman was moving on but now incorporating Rose and Licorice. Our Very Cellular Song was my attempt to write a piece that used as many styles and combinations of the four people's attributes. It's a "trip" through consciousness starting with the domestic and moving through awareness of the spectrum of life's conditions, to a prayer for the wellbeing of all.

Do you have a personal favourite ISB album at all?

When it comes to favourite albums I've always been drawn to songs. So when the songs on an album blend to make a whole experience bigger than themselves, that's a special bonus. And for me Hangman's Beautiful Daughter would be far and away the best example.

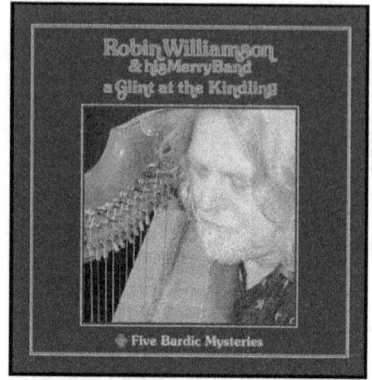

Solo Albums

The solo discographies can at first seem to be a rather daunting place, especially Robin's which features a wide variety, whether they be solo, traditional harp collections, or Grammy nominated collaborations with artists such as John Renbourn or in his Merry Band. Of course there is no perfect starting point, although I found A Glint at the Kindling a brilliant introduction into Robin's versatile solo world. Clearly though, Williamson took a much more traditional approach to his new songs, and Lough Foyle is a brilliant folk number that could have been written hundreds of years ago, with its wonderful jig like rhythm, lush acoustic plucking and violin lines. This sort of Williamson track is vastly under rated, and much more accessible than his more experimental ISB tracks and certainly not lacking his originality and strong character. Another facet to Robin's solo discography is his wonderful story albums set to accompanying light music. Five Bardic Mysteries saw a release in 1981, and was later added as a series of bonus tracks to the CD release of A Glint at the Kindling. It's a lovely set, with Robin's warm tones and fables over soothing harp sounds. The words are wonderfully imaginative too; a great place to start in my opinion. Robin also released one of his most notable solo albums only last year, Love Will Remain, which had shades of his trademark style mixed with tradition. I also found Celtic Harp Airs and Dance Tunes an extremely beautiful album, a soothing listen from start to finish and also a great showcase for his virtuosic harp playing.

Mike Heron's solo catalogue is a much different beast and certainly an easier one to approach as a newcomer than Robin's vast offerings. In fact there are barely 10 solo releases from Mike since the early 1970s. He made his name as a songwriter in the 80s, his songs being covered by a wide range of artists, but he also managed to squeeze in a few very fine solo offerings too.

His first album was the brilliant lost gem Smiling Men with Bad Reputations, released in 1971 while the ISB were still going strong. Produced by Joe Boyd again, it was, as Mike describes it, his idea of a rock oriented album, perhaps music too guitar heavy to feature on an ISB album. One can be distracted of course by the list of famous guests on the album, but can be forgiven for this when taking a look at the names, which include the Velvet Underground's John Cale, Ronnie Lane, Keith Moon, Pete Townshend and Fairport's Richard Thompson. But the songs on the album, although quite different from his ISB numbers, still stand up 40 years later. Even stronger still, quite possibly, is his 1975, first post ISB album Mike Heron's Reputation, certainly a more conventional pop rock album, but showcasing Heron's brilliant vocal talent and song writing knack. Angels in Disguise, taken from the record, could have been written by Cat Stevens in the same era, a truly lovely song with a great arrangement. His best of collection, Echo Coming Back, is also a solid set and an essential purchase for the ISB fan looking to expand their collections into the realms of the solo catalogues.

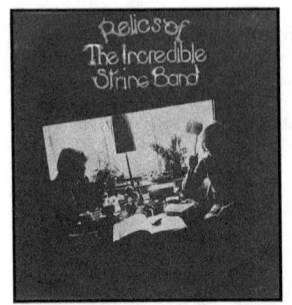

ISB Compilations

Although there are only 12 official ISB studio releases, there are also a number of extra oddities, compilations and live offerings to delve into. Although some bands have their material constantly re-released on budget CD compilations seemingly every month by their money hungry labels, most of the ISB compilations are actually worthy of merit for different reasons.

The first compilation to appear was in 1971 with the release of The Relics of The Incredible String Band, a double LP of stand out ISB tracks. All the standards are here, but we have some unusual ones thrown in too, like Big Ted, the opening track on Changing Horses, plus classic epics like A Very Cellular Song. Less recommended though is the CD release, Introducing the Incredible String Band, which doesn't really represent the band's finest material. In some ways it seemed thrown together.

Much more interesting though are the releases of several BBC recordings and demos, which have surfaced over the last few years. A definite buy is BBC Live in Concert, recorded in 1971 and 1972 with the Heron, Wiliamson, Le Maistre, McKechnie line up, with notable versions of Spirit Beautiful (which was to appear on Mike's first solo release), and a 1972 version of The Circle is Unbroken.

For live releases, Nebulous Nearnesses and Everything's Fine, both recorded in the 2000s, are quite patchy, but the real essential live ISB album is the recently released Fillmore East 1968 CD. Mike and Robin are here on blistering form, shortly prior to the girls joining the line up. The sublime opening version of Waltz of the New Moon is pure ISB perfection, a wonderful sitar line by Heron behind a hypnotic Williamson strum/pluck riff on the acoustic, leading us into the concert ahead.

"It was a key gig," Mike Heron recalled to Folk Radio. "... as it came during a tour in 1968 when the material for the first five Elektra albums was available to me and Robin, prior to the arrival of Likky and Rose. So the songs are intimate and performed as a duo. We'd been touring in the States for six months, and Robin's at the very top of his game – playing hundreds of instruments and being very imaginative. I'm not too bad either but I'm eclipsed by him a bit. I'm really proud of it, how it captures a moment in time."

True, the recording is a stand out in all live recordings by the ISB and it's been floating around on bootleg for years, but the new official release is a must have.

For demo releases, a good addition to the ISB recordings is The Chelsea Sessions, which were recorded in 1967, although its contents are also available on larger collections of rarities, so it may be a bit pointless stumping for that first. Released on Robin's own Pig's Whisker label, the set features some fully realised renditions of classics like the Mad Hatter's Song, Little Cloud and Heron's Lover Man. The sound quality, for a 45 year old demo recording is great too. But if you want to go one further, purchase Tricks of the Senses, a double CD set featuring recordings and rarities from 1966 to 1972. Even better though is 2005's the Circle is Unbroken, Live and Studio 1967 to 1972. It features nothing new (all material had been previously released at this point) but comprises the Chelsea Sessions of 1967 and a live recording of the 1972 line up in Canada. Still, it might be a good place to start if you're looking for live and demo rarities.

Acknowledgements and References

I would like to thank my dad Andy for getting me into the Incredible String Band in the first place (and baffling me with Changing Horses in particular as a kid). Also thanks to Graham Forbes for answering my questions and giving me some great information (his new book Rock and Roll Busker is available on Amazon now), John Hoppy Hopkins, David Snell (who had no recollection of working with the ISB) and Mike Heron himself for taking time out to do the Q and A with me, and also Corrina Seddon for being so helpful. Shout out to the brilliant ISB Yahoo Group too!

The following sources were very useful in completion of this book.

Incredible String Band BBC Documentary
My Mike Heron live review, 2013, appeared in Shindig!
Be Glad Fanzine Archive
Mike Heron Interview with Beat the Retreat
Mike Heron on Radio 2 Folk Show, 2013
Robin Williamson Interview, Swing Time Magazine, 1979
Robin Williamson Interview, Perfect Sound Forever, 2003
Joe Boyd, Guardian Article, 1997
Shamanic Freedom Radio, Robin Williamson Interview
Aylesburyfriars.co.uk
Melody Maker Press Archives
Cash Box Archives
Mike Heron Folk Radio Interview 2013
Scottish Herald Woodstock Article, Graham Forbes 2009
Joe Boyd Interview by Richie Unterberger

Robert Plant, Q Magazine Interview 1993

Pagan Dawn, Robin Williamson Interview, 2012

Whit Bicycles by Joe Boyd

Incredible String Band, Mojo Article

Graham Forbes Rock and Roll Busker, 2013

Hangman's Beautiful Daughter, Rolling Stone review

Beat Instrumental, March 1971

PICTURE CREDITS

Album cover art reproduced is owned by Elektra Records.

Many of the photographers and copyright holders for the images in this book could not be found.

Some photos were also provided by Graham Forbes, who was a great help for completion of this book.

Picture of Lavinia Blackwall and Mike Heron at Hyde Park Cinema taken by the author, 2013

ABOUT CHRIS WADE

Chris Wade is a UK based writer, filmmaker and musician. As well as running the acclaimed music project Dodson and Fogg, he has written books on The Kinks, Malcolm McDowell, Captain Beefheart, Robert De Niro and many others. He has also released audiobooks of his comedic fiction, such as Cutey and the Sofaguard, narrated by Rik Mayall. His other projects include Hound Dawg Magazine, for which he has interviewed such people as Sharon Stone, Donovan and Jethro Tull's Ian Anderson. His art films include The Apple Picker (accepted by Sydney World Film Festival), and he has made documentaries on such figures as Orson Welles, Charlie Chaplin and George Melly.

More info at his website: wisdomtwinsbooks.weebly.com